Heroes of 1960s Motorcycle Sport

Off-Road Giants!

Volume 2

Also from Veloce –

Those Were The Days ... Series
Café Racer Phenomenon, The (Walker)
Drag Bike Racing in Britain – From the mid '60s to the mid '80s (Lee)

Enthusiast's Restoration Manual Series
Yamaha FS1-E, How to Restore (Watts)

Essential Buyer's Guide Series
BMW GS (Henshaw)
BSA Bantam (Henshaw)
BSA 500 & 650 Twins (Henshaw)
Harley-Davidson Big Twins (Henshaw)
Hinckley Triumph triples & fours 750, 900, 955, 1000, 1050, 1200 – 1991-2009 (Henshaw)
Honda CBR600 (Henshaw)
Honda FireBlade (Henshaw)
Honda SOHC fours 1969-1984 (Henshaw)
Norton Commando (Henshaw)
Triumph Bonneville (Henshaw)
Vespa Scooters – Classic 2-stroke models 1960-2008 (Paxton)

General
BSA Bantam Bible, The (Henshaw)
Ducati 750 Bible, The (Falloon)
Ducati 750 SS 'round-case' 1974, The Book of the (Falloon)
Ducati 860, 900 and Mille Bible, The (Falloon)
Edward Turner: The Man Behind the Motorcycles (Clew)
Fine Art of the Motorcycle Engine, The (Peirce)
Kawasaki Triples Bible, The (Walker)
Lambretta Bible, The (Davies)
Laverda Twins & Triples Bible 1968-1986 (Falloon)
Moto Guzzi Sport & Le Mans Bible, The (Falloon)
Motorcycle Apprentice (Cakebread)
Motorcycle Road & Racing Chassis Designs (Noakes)
Off-Road Giants! (Volume 1) – Heroes of 1960s Motorcycle Sport (Westlake)
Scooters & Microcars, The A-Z of Popular (Dan)
Scooter Lifestyle (Grainger)
Triumph Bonneville!, Save the – The inside story of the Meriden Workers' Co-op (Rosamond)
Triumph Motorcycles & the Meriden Factory (Hancox)
Triumph Speed Twin & Thunderbird Bible (Woolridge)
Triumph Tiger Cub Bible (Estall)
Triumph Trophy Bible (Woolridge)
Velocette Motorcycles – MSS to Thruxton New Third Edition (Burris)

From Veloce Publishing's new imprints:

Battle Cry!
Soviet General & field rank officer uniforms: 1955 to 1991 (Streather)
Red & Soviet military & paramilitary services: female uniforms 1941-1991 (Streather)

Hubble & Hattie
Animal Grief – How animals mourn for each other (Alderton)
Clever Dog! (O'Meara)
Complete Dog Massage Manual, The – Gentle Dog Care (Robertson)
Dinner with Rover (Paton-Ayre)
Dog Cookies (Schops)
Dog Games – Stimulating play to entertain your dog and you (Blenski)
Dogs on wheels (Mort)
Dog Relax – Relaxed dogs, relaxed owners (Pilguj)
Exercising your puppy: a gentle & natural approach – Gentle Dog Care (Robertson)
Fun and games for cats (Seidl)
Know Your Dog – The guide to a beautiful relationship (Birmelin)
Living with an Older Dog – Gentle Dog Care (Alderton & Hall)
My dog has cruciate ligament injury – but lives life to the full! (Häusler)
My dog has hip dysplasia – but lives life to the full! (Häusler)
My dog is blind – but lives life to the full! (Horsky)
My dog is deaf – but lives life to the full! (Willms)
Smellorama – nose games for dogs (Theby)
Swim to Recovery: Canine hydrotherapy healing (Wong)
Waggy Tails & Wheelchairs (Epp)
Walkin' the dog – motorway walks for drivers and dogs (Rees)
Winston ... the dog who changed my life (Klute)
You and Your Border Terrier – The Essential Guide (Alderton)
You and Your Cockapoo – The Essential Guide (Alderton)

www.veloce.co.uk

First published in January 2011 by Veloce Publishing Limited, Veloce House, Parkway Farm Business Park, Middle Farm Way, Poundbury, Dorchester, Dorset, DT1 3AR, England.
Fax 01305 250479/e-mail info@veloce.co.uk/web www.veloce.co.uk or www.velocebooks.com.

ISBN: 978-1-845843-23-6 UPC: 6-36847-04323-0

British Library Cataloguing in Publication Data – A catalogue record for this book is available from the British Library.
Typesetting, design and page make-up all by Veloce Publishing Ltd on Apple Mac. Printed in India by Imprint Digital.

Heroes of 1960s Motorcycle Sport

Off-Road Giants!

Volume 2

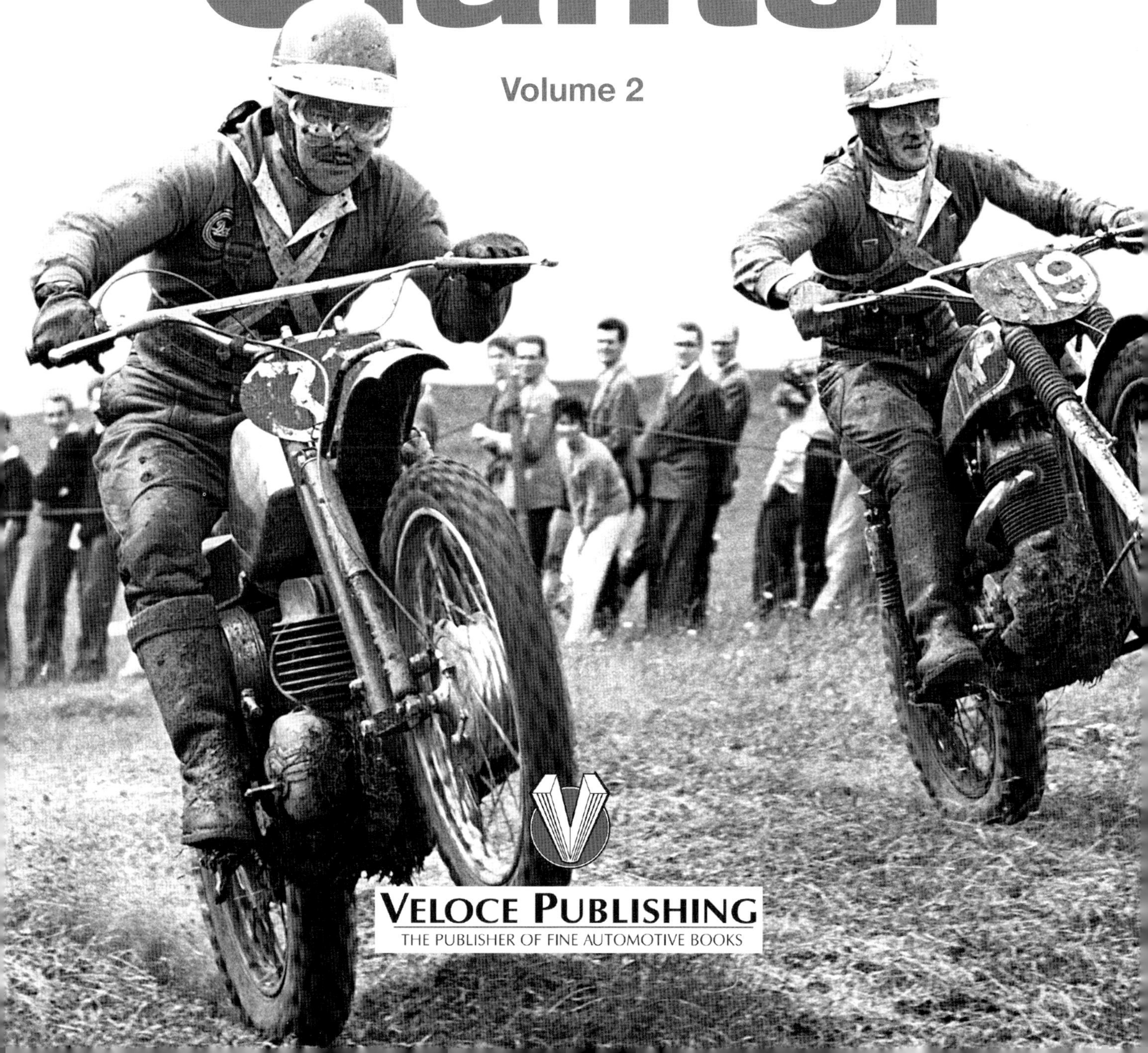

VELOCE PUBLISHING
THE PUBLISHER OF FINE AUTOMOTIVE BOOKS

Dedication

To all the wonderful friends I've met along life's highway.

CONTENTS

Brian Curtis flying on his Matchless Metisse at Farleigh Castle in 1968.

FOREWORD

BY TIM BRITTON

A fact of modern life is the global communications network, which makes virtual contact with anyone in the world almost instantaneous – provided they're on-line, of course. Though it seems we're bombarded with e-mail offers to improve our lives, health, looks or finances on a daily basis by all sorts of people, not all e-mails are unwelcome: amongst the so-called spam are messages from colleagues, family, and friends that *are* welcome. One such email came to me from Andy Westlake, asking if I'd like to contribute the foreword to volume 2 of *Off-Road Giants!*

It's an honour to type a few words introducing the talented riders Andy has featured in this latest edition. If you've not seen volume 1 then you've missed out – just reading through the list of riders is like a trip through competition motorcycling. That Andy has been able to entice more riders to open up about their careers in the golden age of motorcycle sport is little short of incredible, as most considered themselves no different to club riders, and were just having a good time riding. Us club riders knew better though, as we rubbed shoulders with such stars on scramble start lines or waited in queues at trials sections to see their 'line,' in the hope we could do it, too. That is possibly the reason – or one of them at any rate – for the popularity of off-road sport in this golden era: club riders could rub shoulders with the experts in the same events, as we all tackled the same obstacles whichever discipline we were riding.

Of the riders featured in this volume, most have appeared in articles by Andy in *The Classic Motorcycle*, though in *Off-Road Giants! – Volume 2* the words are unedited and supplemented by new photographs to those previously published. What remains the same is Andy's commitment to digging up the juiciest tales from the world of off-road that he and I are so committed to. Like me, he avidly consumed any newspaper report, magazine article or long-lost book about our heroes in trials, scrambles and grass-track, whether on two or three wheels. All of the names in the contents page will be more than familiar to classic and off-road enthusiasts everywhere; after all, they were the headline makers of their time, and some still ride in the classic scene today. Guess what? They're still headline makers.

By the time you've read this part of the book you'll know just who has allowed Andy access to their memories for this particular volume, so I'll not need to repeat the list. What I will say is that each and every one of them has in some way shaped British motorcycle sport, and did it in the days when 'British' meant world motorcycle sport. While some of the riders have stuck to one discipline, others have excelled in several types of event, while others still have managed to combine the rare skills needed to swap back and forth from two and three wheels. All, however, have that rare quality that turns a club rider into a winner, and their paths to success are what make *Off-Road Giants! – Volume 2* such a readable book. So, go enjoy it.

Tim Britton

Editor, *Classic Dirt Bike*

ACKNOWLEDGEMENTS

Many thanks to all the former stars – not only for their help and enthusiasm in compiling these profiles, but also for leaving a young Somerset lad with some wonderful and enduring memories from those carefree days of his childhood. For providing so many images, a huge thanks must also go to Jill Francis (Gordon Francis archive), Morton's archive, and the riders themselves.

Unusual shot of Brian Curtis in a time trial at Yatton near Westbury on a 250cc Greeves in 1961.

John playing to the camera – note the rear suspension on his BSA.

Nicknamed 'Clem' after the 1930s 'bird-man' aerial daredevil due to the amount of time he spent in the air, John Avery generally flew in early 1950s scrambles.

CHAPTER 1

JOHN AVERY - HIGH FLYER

It was said by his old Lancastrian mate Ted Ogden that John Avery spent more time with his Gold Star in the air than on the ground, so it was little wonder that he earned the nickname of 'Clem,' given to him by former AMC ace Geoff Ward in memory of Clempson, the famous bird man of the 1930s, who tried to master man-powered flight with wings strapped to each arm. John might not have had wings, but there is no doubt that the hard riding man from Oxfordshire was one of the most spectacular scramblers of his era, and given his antics on the Small Heath single, the nickname was extremely fitting. On his works-supported BSA Gold Star he was crowned British 500cc scrambles champion in 1952, rode three times in the Motocross Des nations team, and just for good measure, he also found the time in the winter to become an extremely talented one-day trials rider.

In ten dazzling years there was barely a top class event where the name 'John Avery' didn't feature in the results, until a day at Streatley Berkshire in 1957. In a freak accident he was cast off the Goldie, and in the ensuing melee – in which the 380lb BSA landed on top of him - he suffered a badly smashed arm and some nasty lacerations to his face. With a wife and young family to support, plus a busy garage to run, he reluctantly decided to call it a day, thus bringing the curtain down on the Avery scrambling career. It was not, however, the end of John as a top class sportsman. He continued to ride in one-day trials right throughout the '60s, and later on he was persuaded to try his hand at water-skiing. In fact, with skills honed from the days of flying around on his Gold Stars, he became rather proficient at tearing across the water, and in 1975 he won his second national title when he was crowned British senior slalom champion.

It is, of course, as John Avery the scrambler that so many of us remember him best, and it was a privilege to meet John at his beautiful home in Oxfordshire where we relived some of those halcyon days of burnt methanol and Castrol R.

That he should have become a motorcyclist and decide to take part in competition was perhaps not totally surprising. From premises at Headington near Oxford, his father Harold Avery ran a thriving business selling both cars and motorcycles, and in 1933 he and his wife Ida won the British Experts car trial in their rorty Singer Le Mans. John told me a little about those early days and his first bike, which was soon prepared for trials action.

"When I left school I went into my fathers business and soon fell in love with a girder-forked 1939 B21 BSA that had arrived in the

Superb action shot from the early '50s on the works Gold Star (location unknown).

"I WAS DESPERATE TO HAVE A GO AT SOME FORM OF COMPETITION, AND AFTER RIDING THE BSA AROUND THE LOCAL FIELDS AND WOODS FOR A WHILE I TOOK THE PLUNGE AND ENTERED MY FIRST EVENT"

Berkshire Grand National, 1952. John dicing with Brian Stonebridge on his works Matchless.

workshop. With its upswept fishtail silencer it was a beautiful-looking machine and I badly wanted it, so dad agreed that I could have it for £49, which I paid off at ten shillings a week out of my wages. I was desperate to have a go at some form of competition, and after riding the BSA around the local fields and woods for a while I took the plunge and entered my first event: the 1947 Junior Challenge trophy trial run by the Hawks club at Cheltenham. I guess the attraction of negotiating muddy lanes must have been in my blood because both of my parents loved competing in car trials, and prewar had won many events, including the British Championship in their little Singer."

Like many of his contemporaries, John rode the BSA to the start at Cheltenham, where he soon put his many hours of practice to good use. With plenty of feet-up 'cleans' it was a memorable debut from the stylish teenager, who, against some seasoned and experienced riders, scooped the premier award in his very first event. That win in Gloucestershire was the first of many for the talented young Avery, but like most of his generation he was called up for national service at eighteen; although as I discovered, this did little to hinder his burgeoning motorcycling career, with his skills and talents soon being recognised by the army.

"On joining the army I was initially stationed at Ryll in North Wales, but later on I got transferred to the MT school at Boredon where I was an instructor. There were some decent riders during my time there, including Royal Enfield man Josh Berry, and we also had regular visits from AMC's Hugh Viney. At that time Hugh was one of the best trials riders in the country, and he used to come along and give us tips on how to best negotiate all sorts of tricky sections. He certainly helped me, and when I managed to get a 24-hour pass I would ride back home on my Triumph Speed Twin to compete in one of our local events to put his advice into practice. Trials were great, but my heart was in racing, and after I was demobbed the B21 BSA was soon turned into a scrambler. Dad had a BSA dealership so he contacted Small Heath and they supplied us with a set of tele-forks and a 21in front wheel, which gave that all-important extra bit of ground clearance."

Although John didn't set the world alight on his scrambling debut, he was soon on the pace, and following an impressive win in the 250cc race in Cotswold – where he beat works men Fred Rist and Brian Povey – it wasn't long before he was being courted by BSA.

"In addition to the Cotswold I managed to win the 250cc race at the Experts GN, the quarter-litre races at Shrublands Park, and also the Lancs GN on the little BSA. Despite having a rigid rear end the B21 both went and handled pretty well, but I wanted a bigger capacity machine and bought myself a brand new 500cc Gold Star. We fitted it with a Cheshire rear swinging arm – this was a home-brewed affair made by Fred Cheshire in Cheltenham – and in the early '50s it gave me quite an advantage over the riders with the standard setup. The bike was a production alloy-barrelled B34, but the motor was breathed on by Jack Amott and later by Cyril Halliburn, who transformed the power output when we later ran it on dope with an iron head and barrel."

Successes on the B34 saw John selected as a member of the victorious British team in the 1950 Motocross Des Nations event, and with his pair of bikes packed onto his trusty Austin A40 pick-up he travelled thousands of miles to top-line events all across the UK. Spurred on by his wins, he was soon widening his horizons, and 1951 saw him on the road racing against the best riders in the world in his first continental GP in Sweden. In fact, it was almost a dream debut, but he was cruelly denied victory on the last lap when his BSA ground to a shuddering halt.

"I was going like the clappers on my Goldie and leading as I went into the last lap, when all of a sudden the engine stopped dead; seized solid. I pushed it back to the pits where I discovered that a rocker pipe had fractured and it had run out of oil. The rocker pipe was a solid one that was prone to breakage, and to overcome this happening in the future, BSA's 'modification' was to put a piece of flexible rubber between the two ends of metal pipe.

"The standard 500 single was pretty fast, but at the time there was a petrol shortage so Cyril Halliburn tuned the engine to run on dope. This put quite a strain on the motor, and to stop the head lifting I had to put in some extra bolts to hold the barrel down. It was a great engine, which developed power from quite low revs that just increased in a steady flow; it seemed unburstable and I think it was the best motor I ever had."

That same year (1951), the Oxfordshire flyer was again part of the winning British Motocross Des Nations team at Namur in Belgium, and back home in Oxford his newly opened business – buying, selling and repairing motorcycles – was going from strength to strength.

"Before being called up for national service I'd worked with my father in his garage, but when I was demobbed in 1949 he gave me a hand to set up my own business. After the bleak war years everyone was keen to get a bike as their personal transport, and I could sell as many new machines as I could get my hands on."

John's performances on his private Goldie hadn't gone unnoticed at Small Heath, and when John Draper decided to move to Norton, Avery was the man they wanted to fill the vacant seat. His signature was keenly sought by BSA's competition chief Bert Perigo, although as he revealed, it was not the only manufacturer interested in signing him.

"At that time the 500cc Gold Star was the class leader, but Velocette was extremely interested in me riding for them, so before I signed for BSA I went along for a test ride on their 500. Sadly, I quickly discovered that although the Velocette had a super engine, the frame and suspension were truly awful compared to a Goldie. It badly needed a decent set of forks and frame that didn't bend, but the engine had potential, and this was highlighted some years later when Eric Cheney mounted a 500cc motor into a Gold Star frame. It was very impressive, and a bike I owned for a while after I retired from racing in '57."

Although the Velocette frame was not up to the rigours of scrambling, the factory 500cc BSA was an extremely competitive machine, and the '52 season was a memorable one for its rider.

Once again, Avery was a member of the victorious Motocross Des Nations team. Unlike the previous year when his privately-owned Goldie had seized, the works machine carried him to victory in Sweden and countless other major events across the UK. These included the Cotswold, the Sunbeam point-to-point, and the Lancs GN on his works 500, and also many other wins on his privately-owned 250, which was still capable of taking on and beating the rest. By the season's end John had won enough points to be crowned the British 500cc champion; but what was it like to be a works rider back in the '50s?

"By then I'd progressed to a car and trailer that carried the bikes and also a cache of spares, including replacement shock absorbers, sprockets, chains and handlebars in a coffin-shaped box. BSA supplied the bike at the start of the season, but after that it was left very much up to the rider to keep it running. If the motor went sick you could take it back

Flat out cornering on the 500cc Gold Star.

British Grand Prix, Hawkstone Park, 1955. John leads from Reene Barton and Bill Nielson.

to the factory for them to fix, and sometimes at a big national meeting they might send the works truck and some mechanics, but usually the works riders – Bill Nicholson, Basil Hall and me – just fettled our own bikes. I loved the sport, and winning on the works BSA on a Sunday usually generated a sale in my shop on a Monday. In fact I used to buy – and quickly sell – as many as six Gold Star scramblers at a time."

The hallmark of any of Avery machine was its meticulous preparation and immaculate presentation – something which gave him a huge psychological advantage over the opposition – but although his BSA bosses supplied the bikes, John had to work extremely hard to earn any additional prize money from the Small Heath coffers.

"BSA paid me a £50 yearly retainer, and typically at a big national or trade-supported meeting they would put up £50 for a win – but nothing for a place – and of course you would come to the start line alongside the likes of Bill Nicholson, Phil Nex, Brian Stonebridge, David Tye and Brian Martin, who were all after the same fifty quid. Other than events like the Motocross Des nations or the annual north versus south scramble, there were never any team orders and BSA didn't really care who won as long as the first three were all mounted on Gold Stars."

Winning the British title in '52 made John a top attraction for organisers in continental Europe, and during the next four or five years there were frequent journeys across the channel to France and Belgium. They were happy to pay him decent start money, and he quickly became a favourite with the huge enthusiastic crowds who loved his all action, never-say-die riding style on the booming Gold Star. However, there was little opportunity to celebrate as there was always the busy shop to run, which meant a mad dash for the late night ferry back to England.

In addition to his scrambles wins, the name of Avery was a regular one in open-to-centre trials results, but work commitments meant he only rode once in the Scottish six days. In his lone ride in the Highlands – in which he and the 250cc BSA travelled to the start by train – he scooped a first-class award, although his first love was in the muddy lanes of Gloucestershire.

"Compared to the sections in my home county of Oxford, which relied on lots of coloured tape to mark the route, I loved those across the border in Gloucester. This was because they were so natural and there was always plenty of mud about, especially the ones at Draper's Farm, which was always a challenge. The family farm also hosted some wonderful national scrambles, and one of my proudest moments was when I won the 500cc race there in the Cotswold GN on the ex-Draper BSA."

There is no doubt that John was an extremely accomplished one-day trials rider, but his first love was always the speed and excitement of scrambling. Over the years he made good friends with many of his fellow competitors – among them works AMC star Geoff Ward. Geoff was a man who was a fierce competitor on the track, but one who also shared John's keen sense of humour.

"Geoff and I had both entered a fairly small meeting near Builth Wells, where my parents were then running the Boat Inn pub. We stayed overnight, and over a beer Geoff suggested it would be fun to swap bikes for the day. I agreed, and we both had a good days sport with Wardy winning the 500 race on my BSA and me the 350 final on his AJS. When the results were published in the following week's Blue 'un, both Bert Perigo and Hugh Viney thought there must have been some sort of misprint to see Avery on an AJS and Ward on a BSA. However, the truth soon came out and we both got it in the neck from our furious bosses who told us in no uncertain terms that as works riders 'you ride for us and you don't do that.'"

John loved racing in the mud, and one of his favourite tracks was the one that hosted the Lancashire Grand National. Held on the infamous piece of bottomless bog above Bury – referred to by locals as Holcombe Moor – it was a long course of around three miles, with the route marked out across the moor by little flags. The main race was over ten hard laps and always attracted a huge entry, but in the strength-sapping mud the attrition rate was high, and there weren't many who survived to see the finishers' flag – although you could usually bet that Avery and the mud-spattered BSA would be in the leading bunch. John raced his entire career on the 500cc single – undoubtedly 'the' scrambles machine to have in the early '50s – although it was not until the end of the 1955 season that he was able to make those all important improvements to the bike's braking and handling.

"I rode as an official factory rider up until 1955 – the year Janet and I got married – but of course BSA always thought their bikes were perfect, and although they turned a blind eye to minor modifications they didn't want us doing any major alterations to the suspension or braking. By then more of my time was being taken up running the shop, so I decided to relinquish my works ride and bought my bike from BSA to continue as a privateer. The Gold Star engine was superb, and would usually last a full season with little more than a change of oil and plugs and a clean of the contact points, but at 380lb it was a heavy old beast and every other meeting I needed to twist the forks legs 180 degrees to straighten them out. Other than the fitting of a new air cleaner in a box alongside the rear suspension, there had been no improvements to the cycle parts, so my first move was to fit the front forks from a Norton and put a conical hub into the front wheel. It did little to reduce weight, but the bike steered like a train and I could go into corners with the feeling that if needed them, the brakes would bring me to a halt."

For two more seasons John was still able to mix it with the best, but his racing career came to an end on that eventful day at the March Hare scramble at Streatley.

"Landing from a jump the rear suspension compressed, and as it recoiled I was thrown over the handlebars; on my way the valve lifter ripped into my face, and as I hit the ground the bike landed on top of me, breaking my arm in the process. I was pretty badly knocked about, and my father – who had always wholeheartedly supported my racing career – quietly suggested it was time to call it a day. The urge to compete was still there, but scrambling calls for peak strength and fitness, so I decided to take my father's advice. From then on I concentrated my motorcycle sport to winter time trials."

For another decade the name of John Avery regularly appeared in the results of important open-to-centre events, but he rates his best performance as winning a first-class award in the tough Victory trial on a Tiger Cub in 1962.

He finally retired as the Spanish invasion took a hold in the late '60s, but he was never one to sit at home and take things easy, so decided to take up a new sport of water-skiing. The booming Gold Star was replaced by a narrow piece of board, but it was another sport in which the man from Oxfordshire excelled, and one in which 'Clem' truly flew again, gaining his second national title in 1975.

Many thanks to John for his time and hospitality during my visit, and for reliving some wonderful memories from those halcyon days.

'Clem' flying at Draper's Farm in 1955.

Lew with his LCS and just a few of his trophies.

Dorset man Lew Coffin is arguably the best grass-track racer Britain has ever seen – and he continues to be a keen follower of his chosen sport.

CHAPTER 2

LEW COFFIN - GRASS GREAT

There can be few motorcyclists who haven't heard of Lew Coffin, a tigerish, short stocky man from deepest Dorset who was arguably one of grass-tracks greatest ever riders. Beginning his career before World War II, Lew – usually wearing number twenty two – was still winning past master races on his self constructed LCS as recently as 1992. At the age of seventy he was still making it look all too easy, even though he had officially retired fourteen years earlier following a nasty crash at Malvern in 1978, when the chain of his LCS had broken and 'The Killer' had been run over by the rest of the field, multiple pelvis fractures keeping him hospitalised for two long months. To find out more about this crash and the rest of his illustrious racing career, I visited him and his wife of over fifty years, Betty, at their West Country village home: a bungalow named rather aptly 'Creg-ny-Baa.'

In his lounge – or trophy room – is a dazzling array of cups, trophies and mementoes from over thirty years of active racing, with a huge bronze plate taking centre stage. This was presented by the mayor of Osnabruck in recognition of Lew's numerous successes in his 20 years of racing on the German track. Although now aged 86 he still travels to Germany four or five times every year, where he is treated royally by the organisers of the meetings where he registered so many wins. At home in England his jaunty figure is still a regular sight at both classic bike shows and off-road meetings, and in his well-equipped workshop there is usually an engine or two being worked on. He became famous, of course, for his grass-track exploits, but I recall seeing him in action at a Weymouth speedway meeting in the early '60s. At that time I was a ten year old enjoying a summer holiday at the Dorset seaside town, and it was the first occasion I'd witnessed a speedway meeting. Not surprisingly, Lew – who was then in charge of the Weymouth training school – was first past the flag that night. I begin by asking him about his speedway career, where he earned the nickname of 'The Killer,' and how and when he started racing on the grass.

"My dad, who was a farmer, didn't have any interest in motorbikes, but my uncle had a garage selling and repairing cars and bikes, so he gave me one to ride around the farm rounding up the cows. I got pretty good sliding around the fields, and in the summer of 1939 went to my first grass-track meeting near Chard to see what it was all about. I was only sixteen and probably a bit cocky, so after watching the races thought that I could do as well as some of those out there competing, and asked a chap if I could give it a try. Before the ropes

Another good day at a Ringwood meeting in 1964.

In the workshop with his home-brewed 250cc LCS.

were taken down they let me borrow a bike and I tore around for a few laps; I came back to the paddock and they were so impressed they suggested that I give racing proper a try."

On a suitable machine Lew made his race debut in the summer of 1939 at Farleigh Castle, but the clouds of war were looming, and he would have to wait until 1946 before he raced again. This was on a 1928 350cc JAP-engined machine bought for the princely sum of £3 10s; one which, as he told me, had an extremely good motor, but whose handling left a little to be desired. To improve matters, Lew decided to make his own frame.

"The engine had been formerly used by T S Burroughs in his road racer at Brooklands and was a cracker; sadly, on the grass the handling soon showed its limitations, so I decided to ditch the frame and make my own. On leaving school I'd gone to work with my dad on his farm, but it meant being on call seven days a week: something which I wasn't too keen about. After a while I got fed up with this and went working for my cousin Bert, who had a motorbike shop. Bert owned some very interesting machines including an ex-Graham Walker Rudge, which – with no tax or insurance – I rode up and down the country roads. I recall it was a very quick bike, and in fact it's still about and is presently being restored in a village just a few miles from here. With the cutting and welding skills I'd picked up from dad and Bert, I soon cobbled together my first grass-track frame, and it made one hell of an improvement to the standard JAP."

On the special the young Coffin soon notched up his first wins – although not all of his races in those early days were covered in glory. With postwar fuel in short supply, he recalled that the bike was taken to his first meeting at Filton on the train, where from the station to the track was a hard two-mile push. Any temptation to ride the return two miles was curtailed when his engine blew up during the second race. Soon, however, Lew had progressed to a mighty vee twin to transport his bikes to the meetings: an outfit that also became a local taxi for his mates, and quickly became known as 'Old Bill.'

"Of course in those days there were very few cars about, so I bought a big Enfield vee twin to which we attached a flat bed sidecar. Arthur Pullman – who later became British sidecar trials champion – had started racing on the grass, so he and his bike were also transported on the chariot. This meant we ended up going to meetings with three bikes: my two strapped onto the sidecar bed with Arthur's – chain detached – secured by the front forks and towed like a trailer. By then lots of the local lads used to bring their bikes down to dad's farm to practise, and after a while we almost had our own little club running. There was quite a little gang of us, and often on a Friday evening we would climb aboard the outfit and ride into nearby Yeovil for fish and chips; sometimes there were six or seven of us all perched together on Old Bill."

With the skills learnt sliding around on his father's farm, Lew was soon notching up some impressive wins on his home built machines: not only in grass-tracks, but also in scrambles, trials and speedway, in the latter of which he earnt the nickname 'The Killer,' in 1950 ...

"I'd been riding in grass-tracks for about two or three seasons when I read in the paper that Bristol speedway at Knowle were crying out for new riders, so I decided to take my grass-track bike along for a trial ride. They immediately signed me up, but suggested I needed a different bike so gave me a frame – previously been used by Fred Tuck – to house my engine."

Lew was now a speedway rider, and soon delighting the huge crowds with his do or die riding style: sometimes an over-exuberant one, which in an early race resulted in him being the only one of the four starters to finish. This led to him being reported by the meetings steward to the speedway control board, which promptly sent a letter to Lew, signed by Major Fearnley. It makes for some amusing reading:

"... The steward has drawn my attention to your riding at Bristol on June 25th. In event six, in a fit of enthusiasm you bored one rider on the inside of one bend. On the next your riding carried another rider out to the safety fence; and after the steward had switched on your exclusion light you ignored this and carried on, and on the next bend knocked another rider off his machine, again from the inside. I must point out to you that if you ignore the steward's direction in this manner, then nothing but trouble can come of your behaviour. The control board is always glad to recognise enthusiasm in the right place but you must watch your riding carefully in future."

The letter meant that the daredevil Coffin had to curb his full-on riding style, and later that season he was loaned to Exeter where he secured a certain amount of success. So much so he then received an offer to join Yarmouth, but this was turned down largely due to the travelling involved. Grass-tracking was always Lew's first love, although he was also a useful scrambles and trials rider – sports in which he achieved Expert status, and which gave him a huge amount of enjoyment.

"I enjoyed the speedway, but it was starting to interfere with grass-track on which I wanted to concentrate, but scrambles always started earlier in the year than the grass meetings so I built a bike with a JAP engine and had a lot of fun on that. Of course trials were very much a winter activity, and over the years I had several machines including a home-built JAP and a BSA Gold Star. I remember once going full bore up a section on a 250cc Ariel, but disappeared head first into the bushes, at which time a spectator shouted out 'Come out of it Coffin, that's a motorbike you've got there not a bulldozer!' I thoroughly enjoyed all aspects of motorcycling and had some wonderful old bikes on the road, including an ex-Freddie Frith TT Norton, which had no kickstarter or lights and went like an absolute rocket. At that time I was also captain of the Blackmore Vale club who organised road race meetings at the Warminster army camp, where I also raced a couple of times. I recall that Bob Foster used to supply the marshals' bikes, and remember one meeting in which Dickie Dale and I were allocated the job of following the last riders around on their last lap. This was to check that the course was clear, but we started having a bit of a burn up and ended up overtaking several of the backmarkers – something which didn't go down too well with the powers that be in the ACU."

Lew continued to compete regularly in all aspects of sport, and even tried his hand at the wall of death.

"A wall of death was set up in Yeovil, and I went along to look a couple of times. It was quite spectacular, but I thought 'I could do that,' so approached the owner and asked if I could have go. He wasn't too keen as his last man had gone over the top and been killed, but he offered to take me around on the handlebars first to see what I thought of it. I got on OK and rode for about a week under an assumed name – so my parents didn't find out – but got fed up and jacked it in to concentrate on my grass-tracking. My parents were always worried about me racing but my brother was dead keen and used to pay for my entries."

Lew keeps the LCS ahead of Dave Palmer.

"THEY PRESENTED ME WITH THE VICTORY LAURELS AND THE BAND PLAYED THE ENGLISH NATIONAL ANTHEM, I RECKON IT WAS THE BEST MOMENT OF MY LIFE."

Lew at speed at Ringwood in 1962.

Lew might have been only a few inches over the five foot mark, but on the track his strength was awesome, and he was one of the toughest men ever to ride on the grass. He was a great exponent of the foot forward speedway style of riding, and on a damp track Coffin on his LCS – Lew Coffin Special – was virtually unbeatable. Such was his dominance of the sport during the 1950s and '60s he notched up literally hundreds of wins, so trying to pick some highlights is virtually impossible. However, one memorable win occurred on 4 June 1955 – the day Lew married his sweetheart Betty King at Yetminster church. The organist was one of Lew's racing club mates, Wally Monkton, and as the couple emerged from the church they were met by an archway of exhaust pipes and helmets provided by fellow members of the Blackmore Vale club. However, the honeymoon had to be put on hold as the next day Lew was racing at Dunkeswell in the south western centre, where in two exhilarating rides he secured wins in both the 350cc and unlimited cc events.

Not only was Lew a talented rider, he'd also put a lot of work into both the engine and handling departments of his beautifully constructed home-built bikes. With tuning tips picked up from Freshford engine wizard Nells Harring, the 500 JAP was now turning out about 45bhp, and the 350 had springing of Lew's own design. This featured air gun springs contained in the special telescopic front forks, and also had an ingenious rear springing system made up of rubber bands and metal friction dampers.

The 1958 season started as the last one had finished, with Lew winning the Sittingbourne club meeting at Doddington Park, where not only did he defeat national champion Alf Hagon, and Barry Briggs, he also set a new track record of 61.5mph in the process. Wins came thick and fast, including the national inter-centre team races at High Wycombe, the annual Willoughby Hedge Championships – where Lew won the 1000cc final – and rounding off his best ever season with 350 and 500cc race wins at the Broadhembury club's championship event at Willand in Devon. He had also started to spread his wings, making his first race appearance in Germany; the May meeting marked the start of a long and happy association between the hard-riding man from Dorset and thousands of German grass-track fans.

"Fred Parkins and I decided it would be a great experience to race in Germany, and managed to get a ride at an international meeting at Hallsburgh near Minden. We didn't quite know what to expect, but discovered it was a hellishly fast track lined by a crowd of about 40,000 people. There were riders from 13 different countries taking part including the champions of France, Holland, Belgium, Switzerland, Austria and Germany. I had a good ride in the first 350cc race and finished second to Joe Hoffmeister, with Fred Parkins a close third."

In the main 500cc event – cheered on by the huge crowd – Lew put in another scintillating performance and fended off the two crack Germans Alfred Mach and Siegfried Klaus, going one place better to scoop a well deserved victory.

"They presented me with the victory laurels and the band played the English national anthem, I reckon it was the best moment of my life. Afterwards, Fred and I were taken on a tour of honour around the city, and later entertained at a banquet where we were showered with many gifts and flowers."

It wasn't only the Germans who celebrated the famous win, as two days after returning home Lew was interviewed by BBC radio in an interview that, he recalls, lasted 20 minutes or more.

The German organisers and crowds could hardly get enough of the hard-riding Englishman, and over the next five decades he would return on countless occasions. Many of theses rides resulted in Coffin victories, including a memorable one over the then-reigning European champion, Hoffmeister, at Porta in May 1959.

At home Lew continued to notch up a string of race victories, but despite his undoubted talent, he was surprisingly never crowned British champion. This was largely due to the fact that many of the championship finals clashed with events in Germany, which he prioritised. Although he might not have been officially crowned British champion, there were few who could beat the tenacious rider from Dorset. Famous for his rocket-like starts, he won no fewer than nine southern centre 500cc titles, one 250cc and six 350cc championships on top of his numerous wins in Germany. In fact, he recorded so many wins a grass-track enthusiast once told me he came first in more grass races than the great Ulster man Sammy Miller did in trials.

Lew wasn't just a formidable racer, scrambler and trials rider: he has also put a lot back into motorcycle sport. It was largely due to his efforts that the 1000cc sidecars were first taken to the continent, and thanks to his infectious enthusiasm many new bloods went on to become future stars. These were not only grass and speedway riders, but also a young lad from Yetminster who would go on to become one of the world's best scramblers: Brian Goss.

"As a lad, Badger used to come up to the farm and help me clean my grass bikes. He was keen to have a go himself, but Villiers engines were then in short supply, so I built him a bike using a motor out of a DOT ice cream cart. We ran it on dope and called it 'Jet.' It was a pretty quick little bike and Badger rode it in a grass-track, but crashed and broke his leg. He wasn't put off, and his next event was in a scramble at Sturt Hill near Somerton. He fell off in practice, but we got him back on and he went out in the 250cc race and beat Brian Martin on the works BSA. It was obvious he had a lot of talent, and he soon progressed to a works Cotton followed soon after by a factory Greeves. The rest as they say is history!"

Badger was only one of the many that Lew has supported over the years – 20 in 2007 alone – and there can be fewer who have put so much time and enthusiasm into their sport as the stocky man from Dorset.

Certainly for the amount of races he won, history will record the name of Lew Coffin as one of grass-track's greatest, and trying to condense such an illustrious career into a few pages is all but impossible. We finished by taking a trip to his workshops – on view, the machines he was working on for the coming season: superbly functional and competitive bikes, proudly wearing the name of LCS.

Lew Coffin, the people's champion.

A big thank you to Lew and Betty for their time, hospitality and enthusiasm in reliving some of grass-track's wonderful sporting days.

Wonderful action from Yeo Vale in 1965.

With tongue-out concentration on the Cotton in the 1967 Kickham. (Courtesy Gordon Francis)

In a long and varied career, Colin Dommett has spent over 50 years competing in off-road sport – and still retains his enthusiasm.

CHAPTER 3

COLIN DOMMETT - A STUDY IN LONGEVITY

A *Motorcycle News* reporter when he was barely out of short trousers, a works Cotton trials rider by the age of 20, an expert scrambler, ISDT gold medallist and British and European sidecar trials champion ... Colin Dommett was them all. Over 50 years after he rode in his first event he is still able to show the younger brigade a trials trick or two, and it was great to meet up with him at his West Country home to relive some of those halcyon days. Today, Colin is a regular sight and sound around the pre-'65 scrambles and trials scene, but as he recalled, if it hadn't been for summer holidays spent on his cousin's farm at Axminster he might never have become a motorcyclist.

"My father was a farmer and never had any interest in bikes, but as a lad I used to spend all six weeks of the summer holidays at my uncle's farm near Axminster in Devon. My cousins John and George Rutter both had motorcycles, and one summer evening when I was about eleven John asked me if I wanted to go and watch Exeter speedway on the back of his BSA Star twin. I jumped at the chance, and remember vividly the thrill of tearing around a sweeping left-hand bend. It was great, and I decided there and then that when I was old enough I was going to get a bike. John had ridden a bit in trials and scrambles, so they started taking me to watch both scrambles and road racing at places like Blandford and Castle Combe, and I absolutely loved the sights, smells and excitement of it all. Of course in those days there was no schoolboy sport so I couldn't get to compete myself, but when I was aged about fourteen Cyril Quantrill started *Motorcycle News* and somehow I managed to get the position of their sports reporter for Cornwall. We were then living near Truro, so to get to the events I either cycled or stood out on the A30 until I hitched a ride from someone like Ally Clift driving past on his way to compete."

When Colin started riding himself he would often be pictured in the Blue 'un and Green 'un, but he recalled that his photo first appeared in print in the November of 1955.

"Because it was Remembrance Sunday there was no sport that weekend, so to fill space *MCN* ran a feature on all of its contributors, including both me and photographer Gordon Francis, who was also just getting started."

Colin would continue to write his reports for *MCN* until 1964, but by then he was an established trials rider himself, having started in the autumn of 1957.

"On leaving school I'd worked for a while on a farm and then got

Colin, feet up on the rare Cotton-Villiers Starmaker in the mid-'60s. (Courtesy Gordon Francis)

"COLIN TRAVELLED TO EVENTS
THE LENGTH AND BREADTH
OF THE COUNTRY, ALTHOUGH
SOMETIME HE DROVE WITH
TOO MUCH VIGOUR FOR THE

On the 250cc Cotton outfit in the 1965 DK Mansell. The heavily-scarfed man behind observer Gwen Winwood is Bob Currie. (Courtesy Morton archive)

a job at W H Collins motorcycle shop in Truro. I was originally taken on to be an apprentice mechanic, but as I had such knowledge of the British spares they put me in the stores and I never got out. I rode in my first trial in the autumn of 1957 at Colwith Farm near Par in Cornwall, on a Triumph Tiger Cub. It was a proper trials Cub with lights, so I rode it to the start and took the lights off, but during the trial it suffered from a horrible misfire. I managed to finish, and it was only when I rewired the lights to return home I discovered that the primary chain had nipped the alternator wire, causing the misfire."

Colin didn't feature in the results on his debut, but the following week he rode in the St Buryan enduro: a tough time and observation trial, in which the young Dommett gave a good account of himself winning a first-class award.

"By winning the first-class award I was immediately upgraded to Expert status, so it meant that in my entire trials career I never actually won a novice award. Sadly the Tiger Cub was very unreliable, and in the first three months the engine blew up, the big end went twice, and I just didn't have enough money to have it repaired. One of Jack Collins' mechanics, Monty Osborne, did a lot of work on it for me, and I think I probably kept him going in fags as payment, but after about six trials I decided to call it a day and carried on reporting the events for *MCN*. In fact, after competing in a few trials myself this did me a lot of good, as I learnt much from watching how both good and not so good riders tackled different sorts of sections."

After a break of several months Colin was back in action on one of Ally Clift's Villiers-powered ACS, and it was on this Tandon-framed bike that he won his first open-to-centre premier award in 1959.

"It was the East Cornwall club's Kings of Oxford trophy trial, and as a result of this win I was picked to represent Cornwall in the inter-centre team event in Wales. I can't remember much about the trial itself, but I recall that a photograph of me in my Tyrolean style hat appeared in the following week's *Motor Cycling* – a copy of which was on the wall of Adrian Kessel's workshop for the next thirty years."

In his sports reports for *MCN* Colin was never afraid to criticise an event, and as a result he found himself organising his first trial before the age of 20.

"I learnt a lot from Ralph Venables, and in my reports I was never frightened to say if I thought a trial was good or bad. In one I dared to mention the over-use of orange tape to mark the section boundaries, and one of the club's principles told me in no uncertain terms that if I could do better then I should do so. I agreed and a few weeks later I was laying out the sections for my first event. I guess it must have gone OK because less than a year later John Bassett and I found ourselves organising the Trispen Da Cuna, which later in the '60s would become a national."

Not only was Colin one of the Cornish centre's leading trials riders; he also tried his hand at scrambling on one of Ally Clift's Gold Stars.

"In the late '50s Jack Collins was sponsoring Ally Clift on Cotton and a Gold Star, so when Ally was injured I got to ride his Goldie a few times. I did OK, and later in '62/'63 represented Cornwall in the inter-centre team event at Wakes Colne. I remember during the race I was passed either side by Derek and Don Rickman, who went by as if I was stopped. I had a few good scrambles meetings, including one at Haldon Hill where I won £12 – equivalent of three week's wages – on a 250cc Sundry. This was a Sun Villiers with a Vale Onslow conversion, which made it go like the clappers! I continued scrambling up until I got married in 1963, but after a spill I'd suffered a nasty back injury, which meant that although I continued to 'ride' I was reluctant to 'race,' so called it a day at the end of the '63 season."

By then Colin was a riding a works-supported Cotton in trials, although as I discovered, his first ride on one of the Gloucester two-strokes was a long one back to his Truro home.

"David Paul had the Greeves agency in Cornwall, so Jack Collins took on the one for Cotton. It was decided that I would replace my ACS with the latest Cotton trials iron, so I went to Gloucester on the train, collected the bike and rode it home. The factory was a small concern with only about a dozen or so people working there, but everyone was extremely friendly, and Pat Onions told me that if I won an open-to-centre trial they would make me a works rider. I didn't manage to do that, but three or four months later I was invited to ride as part of the factory team in the Wye Valley national."

It was the start of six happy and successful years on the Gloucester two-strokes, but although he notched up numerous wins in his home

Refueling at the 1970 ISDT. Colin and his Cheney Triumph.

Colin showing plenty of feet-up style on the RL Suzuki.

centre, riding in the nationals involved a lot of travelling, so in 1964 Colin was bound for Bristol.

"In the pre-motorway days the trip from Truro to compete in one of the nationals involved a lot of travelling, and I was putting thousands of miles on my car and trailer. I saw a job advertised in the stores at Tim Pritchard's Westbury motorcycles in Bristol, which I applied for and started in early 1964. On the shop's half day I used to travel up to Cottons to collect Villiers engine spares, and on one of my visits – only three months after starting at Westbury's – Pat Onions asked me to go there and work in the stores. Not only was this great geographically for the nationals, I also had Malcolm and Tony Davis as both my neighbours and weekend trials companions. They were two great riders, and I learnt a lot from riding with them."

With the Davis brothers and John Ashcroft Colin travelled to events the length and breadth of the country, although sometime he drove with too much vigour for the local police.

"On our way to one trial I was stopped by the police near Worcester. The officer solemnly told me my mudguards had fallen off the trailer, but he then grinned and said 'I guess it doesn't apply to you because you're flying, not driving,' and sent me on my way."

Although he was a works rider there was little money at Cottons, and Colin recalled that his wife's weekly wage was a welcome supplement to his earnings from the Vulcan Works in Gloucester.

"Cottons supplied me with the bike and spares, but the whole place was run on a shoestring, so there was little in the way of money for expenses. At that time I recall my wife was earning £7 a week, and going to trials seven weeks on the trot cost me exactly £49.

"Monty Denly – who smoked like a trooper – was in charge of the accounts, Pat Onions was works director, and Fluff Brown was in charge of the comp shop and engine development. Because money was so tight they couldn't afford to send me to do the Scottish six days, although I did get to compete in all of the important nationals and British Championship rounds."

Colin was quick to point out that as a rider he was never in the top bracket at a national, but in the early '60s there were some memorable rides, including qualification for the British Experts: a highlight from his days on the works Cotton.

"At that time there were some fantastic trials riders about, and if I got into the top six at a national I considered it to be a great achievement. Of course, when Bultacos came along things got even tougher, and it was hard to get in the top ten."

Colin soldiered on against the tide of Spanish two-strokes until the winter of 1966/'67 when a 'one-off' ride on a Bultaco brought a curt note from the Gloucester HQ.

"I worked at Cottons for about two and a half years before I decided to move back to Cornwall and my old job at W H Collins. By then John Bassett had taken over as *MCN*'s Cornish correspondent and he'd just bought himself a new Bultaco trialer, which he invited me to ride in a Camel vale event. It was the first time I'd ridden a Bulto, but it was miles better than my Cotton and I ended up winning the trial on it. Of course the results appeared in *MCN*, and the following day I received a note from Cotton's which simply read 'please send the bike back, we have plenty of other riders wanting to ride it.'"

Colin would ride the Collins-sponsored Spanish bikes for the next three seasons, but after a change of jobs in 1970 he rode a Greeves Pathfinder, and then another Bultaco for his new sponsor, David Paull.

Colin and Eric Chamberlain on the Suzuki on their way to winning.

During 1971 he notched up numerous trials wins in the Cornish centre on the 250cc Bulto, but after several years of trying he also won his one and only ISDT gold in the Isle of Man.

"I think I'm correct in saying that if you were in the top ten of the British Trials Championship you were invited to take part in the ISDT training sessions, which in 1965 were on the Isle of Man. I was entered on a Starmaker-engined trials bike, but the motor which was being prepared by Villiers didn't turn up at the Cotton factory until 5.00pm on the Friday afternoon, so I had no chance to test it. In the practice event it broke down and I had to pull out. Afterwards I discovered that the condenser lead had sheared and I ran out of sparks. I didn't get to ride in the ISDT proper until 1968, when I rode a Husky for the Vase team in San Pellegrino in Italy, but it was a vicious event and I was forced to pull out when the rear brake plate broke up."

The following year saw Colin on a Collins prepared 500cc TriBSA, and he was going well until the fourth day, when sadly the ignition packed up, bringing another retirement.

Hoping for better things, 1970 saw the Cornishman lined up on a Cheney Triumph as official reserve for the British trophy team in Spain, but after a promising start, his six days ended in spectacular style.

"Before the trial started, Scott Ellis and Johnny Giles gave me plenty of good advice, including: 'If you have a problem, don't do anything until you have looked at your watch.' I remembered this when I had a puncture, and as I didn't have time to put in a new tube, set off again with one of my gloves stuffed inside the tyre and still

At the top of a steep climb in the 1978 Welsh two-day trial.

on time. Later I was tearing along a gravel track absolutely flat out on the Cheney, when I came to a marshal's point where the police were guiding us off the road and through a dried-up stream bed. As I was exiting the stream bed I gave the bike a handful of throttle and did a wheelie, but as I did so the front wheel and the forks fell out and I crashed. We later discovered that the screws which secured the fork stanchions had stripped, so yet another ISDT retirement. I was beginning to think I would never finish an ISDT, let alone win a medal, but in 1971 I was a member of the Bultaco Comerfords/Shell team of Karl Rowbotham and Dave Jeremiah in the Isle of Man. The bike ran absolutely faultlessly for the whole six days, and I came away with a gold medal."

Although Colin was on the shortlist for selection in '72, he was by now running his own business, and due to work commitments he had to pull out. It brought the curtain down on his ISDT career, but little did he realise he was about to enter the most successful phase of his competition life.

"By the mid-'70s I was still riding regularly in the Cornish centre, and I managed to win the centre championships on an Ossa, but I was past my best and not really enjoying things too much. One day I was out making a delivery to a customer who asked me how I was and what I fancied doing next. My off the cuff reply was 'sidecars,' and his response was 'OK, and I'll be your passenger.'"

Colin's customer was Eric Chamberlain, and it didn't take long before the duo made their three-wheeler debut, shortly followed by their first win.

"Eric had an RL 250 Suzuki solo which he donated, and I sorted out a chair before going off to Scotland to ride in the six days on my Ossa solo.

"The Sunday after my return from the Highlands we decided to ride in the Pendenis open-to-centre sidecar trial, and although we didn't figure in the results we had a pretty good ride – Eric was a natural in the chair – and at the end of May we jumped in with both feet and entered the Lyn national trial. Although it was only our second event we did really well, and against a line-up of experienced charioteers, we managed to finish in the top half of the results. The Lyn was held on the Sunday, and the organisers also held a closed to club event on the bank holiday Monday, which many of the crews stayed over to ride in. Amazingly we had a great ride, and when we saw the results we were over the moon: Eric and I were the winners, and we felt we could take on the world."

The pair's undoubted talent was soon spotted by Alec Wright, and it took only one test ride for them to decide to ditch their home-made Suzuki outfit for the latest KT 250 from Kawasaki. It was on this machine they started the winter 1975 season, and on which only five months after their debut ride at Pendenis they would scoop one of trial's biggest prizes: the British Experts.

"After we got the Kawasaki, Eric and I decided we would do as many of the nationals as possible to try and qualify for the '76 Experts. In fact, we managed to get enough points twelve months sooner than we hoped for, so we went off to the '75 event which was held at Rhayader in central Wales. It was a dream ride for us, and it took a bit of time before it really sunk in that we'd gone from rank beginners to British Experts winners in five short months."

The win brought about renewed enthusiasm for Colin, and that same season they rode the little Japanese two-stroke to plenty of other premier wins, including the southern Experts at Asham woods near Frome, and the Cornish centre championships ahead of the previously dominant Rod Dyer. Lightweight two-strokes were now leading the way in sidecar trials, and not wishing to be left behind by their Japanese rivals Beamish Suzuki soon came courting the Cornish pair.

"We started the '76 season on the Kawasaki but Brian Fowler was keen to get us on a Beamish Suzuki so we agreed to ride one of Mick Whitlock's RL-powered outfits for him. Understandably it virtually mirrored the handling and power characteristics of the Kawasaki, and we immediately felt at home on it. We competed in all of the British Championship rounds that year, and at the end of the season Eric and I were crowned champions. Although Eric was no great solo trials rider he was an outstanding passenger, and I couldn't have wished for anyone better in the chair. He was always very relaxed, had a great sense of balance, and seemed to have a natural feel for when the rear tyre was about to break traction."

That chance remark Colin had made while delivering stock certainly paid dividends, because the pair would go on to win the British Championships three years on the trot – '76, '77, and '78 – and also the European title in 1977. The Beamish Suzuki outfits took six out of the top ten in the British Championships in '78, but due to family and work commitments Eric decided to pack up, which meant that Colin lined up for the '79 season with a new passenger and a new bike.

"Comerfords were keen to have me on a Bultaco, and Oriel Bulto even managed to secure some money from the Spanish government to help finance our title challenge. Harry Foster made the chair – in which Ally Clift's son Rob took over as my passenger – and we had a decent season, eventually finished fourth in the championships. By then I was seriously thinking about retiring; however, Reg May at Comerfords persuaded me to stay on for another season, and with Eric back in the chair for the important events we won the title again in 1980 on the 340cc Bultaco. Comerfords were great people to ride for, and all of our agreements were done on the strength of a handshake."

It was Colin's last British title, but not the end of sidecar trials, as he and Eric rode a Fantic for a couple of seasons. It looked purposeful enough, but it didn't handle as well as the Suzuki, and after four disappointing championship events he decided to call it a day.

"We rode the Fantic in that year's British Experts, but it was hard work, and as we came back over the Tamar bridge into Cornwall I threw my boots over the side and said 'That's it, I've retired.'"

It brought the curtain down on five memorable championship seasons, but for Colin trials was a hard drug to give up, and during the mid-'80s he and Rob Clift continued to make the occasional appearance on a JASO (just another Suzuki outfit) in Cornwall centre events. In fact, it's probably safe to say that Colin Dommett has never truly retired from motorcycling. In 1990 he started scrambling again on a potent Triumph Metisse – this finally pensioned off in 2000 – but trials continue to this day, and there are always a couple of pre-'65 irons – presently a C15 and a 250cc Cotton – that in his expert hands see plenty of winter time action.

There's no doubt that the man from Truro was one of the West Country's most talented and popular riders of his generation, and it was a pleasure to relive some of those magical days with him.

Big thanks to Colin and his wife, Greta, for their time and hospitality during my visit.

1948 ISDT, San Remo, Italy.

CHAPTER 4

BOB RAY - ARIEL ACE

Signed straight from his World War II 'demob,' Bob Ray was a mainstay of the Ariel works team through much of the 1950s.

In the long history of off-road motorcycle sport, there can be few riders who secured a works machine before they had ridden in their first major competitive event. However, one individual who did was a young man from north Devon, Cecil (Bob) Ray. Immediately after the war, surprisingly Bob was signed by Ariel to compete in trials scrambles and international six day events, although at that time most of his off-road motorcycling had been conducted in khaki army green.

In the early days of World War II he'd been stationed at Denton Moor for training, and it was here that he caught the eye of his army instructor – and civvy street trials ace – Jack Williams. The moor was a bleak, rough and often muddy stretch of land that Williams would ride across at high speed on his army issue BSA, leaving the hapless squaddies floundering in his wake. When suitably well ahead, he would stop and wait for his breathless beginners to catch up. However, one day when he stopped he discovered he was not alone – following closely in his wheel tracks was the young Cecil Ray. Needless to say, Williams was suitably impressed, and six years later, when Bob was de-mobbed, his co-instructor, Jimmy Edward, persuaded Ariel that Bob was the sort of rider it was looking for, and should sign him immediately. Tommy Davis – director of Ariel Motors – liked what he saw, and quickly signed him as an official member of the works team. It was the beginning of a great career.

Despite the postwar austerity, people were keen to return to some sort of 'normality,' and as early as 1946 Bob was pitched into both trials and scrambles action on the Ariel single.

One of the first trials was an extremely muddy trade-supported Colmore; a difficult event in which Ariel's new boy lost a lot of marks, but one in which he showed plenty of potential. It was a tough baptism, but he learnt quickly, and over the next 12 years would become one of the best trials, scramble, and international six days riders of his generation.

Bob Ray was born on the last day of World War I, and ninety years on still lives in the north Devon town of Barnstaple, a busy town where he spent much of his life running a successful motorcycle business – one that, not surprisingly, specialised in Ariels.

50 years might have passed since Bob hung up his black Barbour suit for the last time, but as I discovered, he still has some great memories from those halcyon days of motorcycle sport. It was a great privilege to be invited along to talk to him, and I started by asking how

he first got interested in motorbikes, and how he became so useful at speeding across rough and muddy countryside.

"My father was a farmer just outside of Barnstaple, and although he had no great interest in motorcycles he owned an old 350cc Ariel which was used for rounding up the cows and as a general workhorse on the farm. From an early age I used to tear around on it, and soon developed a real flair for riding over rough ground. I was a territorial when I was called up in the early days of WW2, and because I did well on the training grounds I spent the next six years instructing the soldiers on how to ride and maintain their bikes; something which was both extremely interesting and rewarding. Later I was taken on as 'staff' and based at Keswick with a good set of top riders including 'Crasher' White, Freddie Smith, and Ariel man Alfie West. The Keswick course was quite demanding, and often the raw squaddies would stop and scream when they came to the top of one of the steep drops. When the war was over I was demobbed and got an offer from Ariel director Tommy Davis inviting me to ride one of their works bikes; as you can guess, it didn't take long for me to say 'yes please.'"

As previously mentioned, Bob didn't set the trials world alight on his ride in the 1946 Colmore, but he was soon picking up first-class awards, and also displaying his prowess on the scrambles tracks. He was a member of the victorious south western team, which won that year's north versus south scramble, and in the December he won his first trials premier award. Not an insignificant club or open-to-centre event, but the biggest one in the trials calendar: the British Experts at Stroud. In doing so he beat the cream of the trials world, including all of the established stars such as Fred Rist, Jim Alves, Hugh Viney, Charlie Rogers, Alan Jefferies, and Bill Nicholson.

Like most aspiring trials stars, Bob rode his Ariel to events all across the south west, but later he bought himself a Standard Vanguard car to which he attached an 'across the boot' bike-carrying rack. Similar racks are now commonplace for trials bikes, but Bob could probably claim to be the inventor of this system; something he devised after being nicked for speeding with his trailer.

"Riding in events all across the country involved driving thousands of miles a year, and I got fed up with continually being fined for speeding with my bike on a trailer. I figured that if I made a rack across the back of the Vanguard the bike would travel OK, and I could also make a bit of a nose-thumbing gesture to the constabulary."

The Ariel – 56in wheelbase, girder forks and steel petrol tank – was undeniably a heavy old iron, and perhaps not ideally suited to the rigours of scrambling, but in Bob's hands it featured in some memorable events during 1946 and '47.

"I managed to win the huge Patchquick trophy in 1946, but the bike – a rigid framed 500 – had quite a bashing, and by the time I finished the footrests were very bent and twisted. As a result of this win I was selected to ride for the British A team in the first ever Motocross Des Nations event, held near The Hague in Holland."

After the rigours of six years of war, thousands of fans enthusiastically lined the sandy track and witnessed a truly fantastic day's racing: one in which the British team of Billy Nicholson, Rist and Scovell (BSAs), and Ray and Stocker (Ariels) managed to hold off a determined Belgium B team to win the victors' laurels by a mere nine seconds. A slightly fortunate win, as it transpired, as near the end of the race Bob's layshaft broke and he had to ride the last lap in top gear.

During his years in the army Bob had displayed a flair not only for riding motorcycles, but also for keeping them up and running, so in '46/'47 he decided to put his skills to the test and opened his first shop. This was in his home town of Barnstaple, and it proved very successful – so much so he later opened further outlets in Braunton, Ilfracombe, and Tiverton, although he added "It was hard work, and perhaps looking back I should have stuck with one or two shops instead of four."

It was a tough time to start a business. 1947 had started with a prolonged cold spell that brought heavy snow and ice, and a government that nationalised everything in sight. The combination of the bad weather and governmental dithering saw acute coal shortages, which in turn brought about compulsory industry shut downs, bread rationing, and withdrawal of the 'basic' petrol ration. Undoubtedly difficult times, but trials organisers somehow kept the sport running, and Bob told me a little about that year's Scottish: his first ride in an event that would become one of his favourites in the feet-up calendar.

"I loved riding in Scotland, although I recall that because of the petrol rationing in 1947 the organisers had to shorten it, although it was still a tough event. I was doing pretty well until day three and the section at Kinlochourn. This was about a mile long, divided into eight sections with 19 hairpins, while the upper parts had a one in two gradient with a surface of solid and loose rocks, mud and shale. I was clean up to section five, and then something went wrong on a left turn over some loose rocks. I didn't have much ground clearance on my Ariel and I shuddered to a halt for a five."

Despite this stoppage Bob pressed on, and at the end was rewarded with the over 350cc cup, sharing the club team prize with winner Hugh Viney and Jack Blackwell. During the next decade he would pick up many first-class and 500cc cups in the Highland classic, but against a plethora of top feet-up stars like Viney, Gordon Jackson, and Billy Nicholson, that outright premiership win would always just elude him.

Like the Ulsterman Nicholson, Bob also got quite a reputation for his ability to attack a tough section at speed, and he laughed as he told me about his policy of "taking it flat in second."

"In those days the trials Ariel was fitted with quite a fierce cam, which meant that it wouldn't 'plonk' as well as a BSA; in fact, it was quite a handful, especially in some of the sections in the Scottish. They were also pretty heavy bikes, so if I was any doubt about its ability to get up the section it was a mater of putting it in second and revving it flat out for as much as the old engine would allow. Ariel's were a friendly crowd to work for, but they wouldn't experiment too much, and were loath to spend much money on developing the bikes. A lot of the time I was with them I rode the bike registered GOV 131, but the number had been around for years, and they just took it off one bike and put it onto the next season's new machine. For a while I also rode GOV 132, which of course is the number made famous by Sammy Miller, who took over my works ride when I retired. Selly Oak supplied my bikes, but although I was a works rider there was little or no money involved; the only 'extras' came from Lucas, Renolds chain, or from the oil people if you won a trade-supported event or if you did well in the Scottish. I took the bikes back to the factory every couple of weeks for them to overhaul the engines, although when I started riding in the international six days they supplied me with a new bike each time."

As he had already demonstrated in scrambles, Bob was more than capable of riding a bike at speed over rough terrain, so his fast but smooth style was ideally suited to the rigours of the ISDT. On Ariel

Scottish six days trial, 1952.

In action on the Welsh.

singles and twins he would go on to ride in eight ISDTs, winning several gold medals along the way, but in his first event in Italy in 1948 he had to survive a collision with a lorry and a nasty last day crash before winning his gold. In the first incident his footrest and front brake lever were badly bent after coming together with the truck, and later on a tricky mountain hairpin he had to lay the bike down to avoid a multiple pile-up after Ellis had gone over an unguarded drop and Bandirola had fallen whilst avoiding him. It was an impressive ISDT debut, which meant that the following year Bob lined up for the 24th international at Llandrindod Wells as an official member of the British trophy team.

In unusually dusty conditions he was on gold medal schedule until the Thursday, when after missing a turn he had to make a Herculean effort to recover lost time. In doing so the Ariel's brakes faded badly, and with little or no stopping power he hit a car and dropped his time card. He managed to retrieve the card and clocked in at the next control, but he was seconds over time. This meant a loss of marks, but thankfully there were no further mishaps, and at the end of six hotly contested days the British trophy team of Viney, Rogers, Ray, Rist, and Jim Alves was declared the outright winner.

In numerous trials, scrambles, and internationals, the name C M Ray figured in the results. But how did he become known as Bob?

"I'm not really too sure, but it's a name I had right back to childhood. Somebody once told me it was because as a kid I was always bobbing up and down around the house, but your guess is as good as mine."

International gold medals are very special, and Bob remembers with great fondness one of his best performances, which came as a member of the 1950 British trophy team, this time on a Red Hunter twin. Based once again in central Wales, it is remembered by those who took part as being tough and very wet; in fact, some experts said it was as strenuous as San Remo in 1948, and as wet as the Lake District in 1927. The conditions were truly awful – 20 yards visibility for the final day's speed tests at Eppynt – but the British riders were in scintillating form: their bikes ran faultlessly, and after six hard days both the trophy and Vase A teams remained completely unpenalised, a fantastic achievement. It was a great year, as in addition to his ISDT gold Bob won the Kershaw Cup (for best under 500cc) in the Colmore, and also won the Raspin bowl in the Scott trial. He was actually best on observation, but was beaten by a single mark by BSA man Nicholson, who recorded his fourth win in five years. The fact that Bob managed to finish the trial at all was quite remarkable, as he negotiated much of the 60-mile Swaledale course nursing an oil-starved engine after splitting an oil pipe on the Ariel single.

There were also some good scramble wins, including the Lanc's Grand National, the Patchquick trophy again, and a memorable victory over fierce rival Geoff Ward at his favourite Farnham circuit in Hampshire.

"I enjoyed scrambling the Ariel, but it was a heavy old beast and not that easy to race; things broke fairly regularly, but when it kept going I had some decent results including a few wins on the continent."

Throughout his career Bob stayed loyal to Ariel, although he recalled once being severely chastised by his boss – this after he'd innocently blagged a test ride on one of the 'opposition's' machines.

"One of my pals had just bought himself a new 500T Norton, and asked me if I would like to try it out in a trial. It was only a local closed to club event, and I guess that if I hadn't won then nobody would have been any the wiser; certainly Tommy Davis wasn't at all pleased, and I was severely dragged over the coals for riding another manufacturer's bike."

For the young Ariel man, travels to mainland Europe in the early 1950s left some lasting memories, especially those to venues behind the Iron Curtain.

"The bikes were taken to the international six days in the official BSA works van while we were left to make our own way. I remember going to one event in Czechoslovakia in my Vauxhall Victor, which was painted in a horrible colour, and all of the locals thought it was a government vehicle. Most of the ordinary people made a real fuss of the riders and were extremely friendly, although we were watched and tightly controlled everywhere we went. People would come up for a chat as they looked upon us as from the 'free world,' but they had to be very careful as almost every other person seemed to be a government informer. The trial itself was extremely well organised, although with

ISDT 1952 – Bob Ray (183) chasing 131 and 51 near Mandling.

"IN HIS FIRST EVENT IN ITALY IN 1948 HE HAD TO SURVIVE A COLLISION WITH A LORRY AND A NASTY LAST DAY CRASH BEFORE WINNING HIS GOLD"

Scottish six days, 1954.

Bob Ray on his Ariel twin – 1955 ISDT, Gotwaldov.

the war only just over the Czechs were very hostile towards the German riders, including George Meier, who would often come to us for a chat.

"The Jawa and CZ 250cc two-strokes were much faster than our 500s, but 80 per cent of the secret of getting a gold medal was simply down to good machine preparation and the ability to make the bike last. Scramblers who competed in the ISDT often didn't last the distance simply because they tried to ride too fast and were too wild."

The Ariel man certainly had a knack for keeping his machine running, and his only ISDT retirement came about on his second visit to Czechoslovakia, when, in a very wet event, some grit got into the carb, causing the throttle to seize.

Compared to the Eastern Bloc two-strokes the Ariel was a heavy, cumbersome beast, and it speaks volumes for the calibre of its riders that it stayed competitive for so long.

On the sprung-frame prototype HT 500, Bob picked up a first-class award in the 1953 Partland Cup. It was to be this bike – GOV 131 – that he would ride until his retirement five years later.

"I think it was 1958 when I decided to call it a day. My form had been slipping, and I knew it was time to get out. Ariel had just signed Sammy Miller – who went to work for them full time – and I then concentrated my efforts on running my four shops, although I still competed in the MCC long distance trials, which I loved."

It brought the curtain down on Bob's highly successful works career, but it's sad to reflect that by the time he called it a day, Ariel was so strapped for cash that it couldn't afford to give him his old bike as a 'thank you' for his loyalty and achievements.

Later – on four wheels – Bob became British production car trials champion, and just for good measure found the time to organise one of the BBC's first televised scrambles in north Devon.

Bob Ray: a gentleman and true champion, who passed away on 28 April 2010.

Many thanks to Bob for all of his time and enthusiasm helping me relive some of those memorable days of off-road sport.

One of Brian's first rides on the 350cc Matchless, aged 18, at Bulbarrow Hill in 1959.

Quiet and modest, Brian Curtis nevertheless established himself as one of the top level scramblers in Britain in the mid-'60s, all the while as a privateer.

CHAPTER 5
BRIAN CURTIS

It was the summer of 1957, and aboard his Francis Barnett trials bike a young Warminster man made the ten mile journey 'across the border' into Somerset. His destination was the Leighton scramble course for an event that was both the inaugural meeting at this now-famous circuit, and also his own race debut. The lad was Brian Curtis, and in the years to come, Leighton – with its steep hills and tricky curves – would become one of his favourite venues. However, as he helped prepare the track that day in '57, little could he have imagined that in a few short seasons he would become one of the West Country's leading scramblers, or that by 1964 his immaculately prepared Matchless Metisse would be taking him to victory in the prestigious Rob Walker trophy at the same venue.

Brian – a quiet and modest man – is from the old school that raced purely for the enjoyment of the sport, but as many of his rivals rapidly discovered, he was both a tenacious and extremely talented competitor. Throughout his racing career he never sought sponsorship or fame, but at the height of it in the mid-'60s there were few who could beat him. In some memorable races he notched up victories against top-class opposition that included many of the country's leading stars, like the Rickman brothers, the Sharps, Ivor England, and Bryan (Badger) Goss.

Not only was Brian a very successful competitor, he later became a highly respected frame builder – a skill that was recognised by the likes of the Rickman brothers, Eric Cheney, and Jack Difazio. In fact, he would go on to produce his own top quality motorcycle and BMX bicycle frames – products that he is still involved with to this day.

In his days on the scrambles track, he had the distinction of being the only man to represent three different centres in the inter-centre team races, and he became known as perhaps one of the best riders of his era never to win a major championship. I first saw him in action in a Bath club scramble in 1962, but it wasn't until the BBC *Grandstand* series hit the Saturday afternoon TV screens that the name of Brian Curtis spread to a nationwide audience. In fact, for a while he had his own unofficial fan club. To find out more about both his successful racing and frame building career, I journeyed to the Somerset market town of Frome to meet this unassuming man.

I began by asking him about his background to motorcycling, and how it all started.

"My dad didn't ride a bike, but in the mid-'50s he took me to a Tor club scramble at Yarley to see some of the West Country's best like Len Saunders and Roy Bradley in action. I was only in my early teens and absolutely loved it; in fact, I decided there and then that when I was old enough I wanted to give it a go. In those days there was no schoolboy sport, so I had to wait until I was seventeen before I could race, although in the meantime I'd spent a load of time riding an old bike around my cousin's farm. I bought a Francis Barnett trials bike and entered my first event at Leighton. It was also the first scramble to be held there, so I rode the Barnett the ten miles or so from home to the track and helped bang in some poles before racing. The only concession to preparing the bike was the removal of the silencer and letting a bit of air out of the tyres. I managed to finish my races, but on the way home the throttle cable snapped and I had to complete the journey with a pair of pliers operating the cable."

Brian continued to 'ride and race' the Francis Barnett for the next season, but it was obvious that the little two-stroke was never going to be competitive, so he delved into his savings and bought himself a new 350cc Matchless scrambler.

"I was working as an apprentice agricultural engineer, and managed to save up enough to buy a 350 Matchless from Difazio's in Frome. I decided on a Matchless because my great hero was AMC works rider Dave Curtis, and chose a 350 simply because I could get more races for my money in a day's sport. I actually registered the bike for the road so I could run it in, and fitted a pair of drop bars pretending to be a road racer, although by then my cousin had bought an A35 so we took both our bikes to the meetings on a trailer. On a Sunday morning before racing I would get very nervous and the only thing I could eat would be a couple of eggs beaten up in milk. That would be my food for the day until the racing was over and I could relax with a sandwich."

Brian raced the 350 Matchless all around the West Country, and people started to take notice of his smooth and fast riding style. After two seasons he'd won enough points to be upgraded to Expert status.

"I'd then bought a Bedford van to transport the bike and managed to score a few wins. Perhaps my greatest moment during that time was when – still as a novice – I managed to beat Len Saunders in an open 350 race at Bulbarrow Hill. Funny thing was, the established experts like Len and Roy Bradley thought I was a bit of an upstart and didn't speak to me. That was until a meeting at Farleigh Castle, when Len and I were both aiming for the same point on a corner and I hit him off. Although Len wasn't very happy at being knocked off, he took it well, and from then on he always had a friendly word with me."

Brian's polished riding style was earning the respect of all of the established Wessex and southern stars, including Ivor England, who was always willing to drop a word or two of advice to the young Curtis. From the 350 Matchless he progressed to a 250 Greeves, and then to a 500 BSA Gold Star, but he didn't like either the two-stroke or the Goldie. His riding skills had not gone unnoticed, and he was soon mounted on a Matchless Metisse, courtesy of Harold Wakefield: a man who supported not just the Rickman brothers, but many other leading West Country riders during the '60s.

"Pretty much out of the blue Harold Wakefield approached me and asked if he could give me some money for a Metisse and a new tow car. He was very generous and later on he also got me a 250 Bultaco, but I could never get on with two-strokes so after a while I gave it back to him for someone else to ride".

It was during this time that Brian's welding skills were noticed, and he landed a job working for the Rickmans at New Milton.

"I can't honestly remember how I managed to get the job at Rickmans, and although at that time I could weld OK I didn't have a clue about brazing. Peter Pykett was also working for Don and Derek, and he taught me how to braze; he was a good teacher, and little by little he gave me more difficult jobs to do until I was good enough to make the whole frames."

Brian was a quick learner in both his racing and his work and he told me how he had improved his riding skills.

"When I started riding I didn't have much of a clue but my secret was to wait to be lapped and then tag on to the back wheel of one of the top riders. It's amazing how much you can learn about the best lines to take and how to keep up a decent pace when you're following a good rider. It also made me realise that to keep up a good race long speed you needed to be pretty fit. Being fit also helps avoid getting injured and in the thirteen years I raced my worst injuries were a broken bone in my foot and concussion after I got knocked in a crash during a team event at Farleigh Castle.

When I went to work for Derek and Don I was there at the same time as Calum Barney, Colin White and Eddie Burroughs all of who were good open-to-centre racers. On Monday mornings we would look around to see who turned up and who had been injured during the weekends racing; during those days I virtually ate, drank and slept scrambling".

Working for the Rickmans, fans naturally assumed that Brian was a factory-supported rider, but other than the first Matchless Metisse supported by Harold Wakefield he bought all of his own machines and had to pay for all of his own spares. Certainly the hallmark of any Curtis machine was that it was always immaculately prepared; something that gave the Wiltshire man a psychological advantage over the opposition long before the starting flag dropped.

As he proved many times in the mid-'60s, Brian was more than capable of taking on and beating his New Milton bosses, but as he told me, racing for him was for the enjoyment of the sport, not just the winning.

"I used to travel to the meetings with my mate and mechanic Cedric 'Zeke' Marsh in my Wolsley car and trailer. Zeke was my general helper seeing to all of the fuel levels and tyre pressures, but I always did all my own spanner work. We did some nationals like the Hants GN and Hawkstone Park, but most of the time I raced in the Wessex, southern and south western centres. Where I lived in Warminster it's right on the borders of these three centres, so at different times I was lucky enough to represent all of them in the inter-centre team events. I think I'm correct in saying that I'm the only rider ever to do that. I actually won enough points in national events to get my international licence, and perhaps my biggest disappointment from my career is that I didn't get the chance to ride abroad. I tried to get some rides, but discovered it to be rather cliquey and couldn't get an entry for love or money. In fact, the only time my face was seen abroad was in the advertising poster for a race meeting in North America – the promoters used one of Gordon Francis' photos of me leaping my Metisse over the hill at Bulbarrow, over 3000 miles away.

"I rather hoped that I might get some sponsorship from Don and Derek but whenever I broached the subject they would say 'I'll have a word with my brother and get back to you.' They might have discussed it but nothing ever materialised in the form of bikes or spares."

Although there was no sponsorship coming from the Rickmans,

Weymouth scramble on the 500cc Gold Star in 1962.

Bulbarrow Hill on the Matchless Metisse in 1963.

Brian did manage to land a one-off ride on a factory BSA in a very muddy Cotswold Cup event.

"I was asked by BSA if I would try one of their factory's 250s in the Cotswold scramble, but on the day it was hellishly muddy. In the melee at the start I dropped the Beezer, breaking the front mudguard, and got my eyes filled with Cotswold mud. This finished my day's racing, and I ended up in the ambulance not being able to see a thing".

During the mid-'60s the combination of B Curtis and his Matchless Metisse was a formidable one, and he continued to notch up an impressive amount of wins; these well reported in the weekly motorcycle press. A typical headline from the 3 July, 1965 edition of *Motor Cycling* read: "The workers have revolted; Brian Curtis puts it across his boss Don Rickman."

This after Curtis had defeated the younger Rickman at the Frome club's meeting at Longleat the previous weekend. Another headline reported that after a race-long dice with Jerry Scott, Brian had scooped the prestigious Rob Walker trophy after his rival crashed his Cheney BSA through the ropes.

In that race Brian was mounted on his tried and trusted Matchless Metisse, but he was looking for a new challenge, and some time later left the Rickmans to work for Eric Cheney. Proud to be associated with what he was helping to construct, he changed to a Cheney 440cc BSA – but as he told me, working for Eric put a lot of miles under the wheels of his car.

"At that time I had a workshop at Longleat, so I would make Eric's frames there and make regular trips to Fleet in my RS Escort rally car to deliver the finished work and pick up new stock. I worked on all sorts of interesting stuff for Eric: not just scrambles frames, but other things for trials and road bikes. I stayed with him for about three years and was still riding regularly myself.

"I can't remember exactly when I finished racing, but I recall one Sunday in 1970 or '71 and I was driving to a meeting and felt no sense of excitement. It had ceased to be fun anymore, so I decided there and then to call it a day. I finished working for Cheney's and set up a workshop next door to Jack Difazio's shop in Frome. Jack was by then really getting into his hub centre steering bikes, so I was involved with him brazing the frames and swinging arms."

Although Brian had given up racing himself, his talents had not gone unnoticed. He was approached by NVT, which asked him to make some frames for the Aberg replicas it had been asked to construct.

"NVT had been asked by the Japanese to make some Aberg replicas, so they approached me to make the frames for them. By then I'd moved to a workshop on the west Wilts trading estate, and over the next two years I made around 400 Aberg replica frames. When this contract finished I concentrated on making some frames of my own. These included one that was fitted out with an XR 500 Honda engine, on which I sponsored Rob Taylor. Rob was a good rider, and he raced it to 2nd place overall that year – 1981 – in the Haynes Four-Stroke Championships."

In total Brian would make some 20 motocross frames, including one powered by a Suzuki SP 370 for trail riding and two more for the road. Ten of these were sold to a customer in Sweden who was keen for him to develop a single shock version; sadly, however, he never came up with the promised financial backing and the idea died a stillborn death.

Demand for scramblers was on the decline, so Brian adapted his skills from constructing motorbike frames to the burgeoning sport of BMX.

"BMX was starting to take off and I decided to make one or two, which although they looked like miniature motocrossers were pretty awful to ride. I soon got it sorted though, and later sold many hundreds of frames around the world, and even ran my own Curtis BMX team. After a while the appeal of BMX died out, and I went working for a company called ABM Airspring in Westbury doing general welding. In fact, I lost all interest in both motorcycles and BMX for many years, and it wasn't until very recently I got back into motorcycling again; this was largely due to scrambles fanatic Dennis Mapp who contacted me and asked if I would be interested in making some more twin shock frames with him."

Wonderful action shot on the Matchless Metisse at Longleat in June 1963.

"IN THE MELEE AT THE START I DROPPED THE BEEZER, BREAKING THE FRONT MUDGUARD, AND GOT MY EYES FILLED WITH COTSWOLD MUD"

Farleigh Castle on the 500cc Matchless Metisse in 1968.

One of Brian's last rides on the Cheney Ducati, at Farleigh Castle in 1969.

The net result of that phone call is that in a little workshop near Farleigh Castle, Curtis frames are being made again. Interestingly, it's just a stones throw from the circuit where, in 1964, one B Curtis won the first ever west Wilts Maybug trophy scramble.

Dennis sees to all of the tube bending and cutting, leaving Brian to weave his magic on the brazing front – a collaboration that suits both men admirably. Without compromising the hand-built nature of the product, the pair now use laser-cut engine plates – the originals would have been all flame cut by Brian – and top quality brazed T45 tubing, as opposed to the original Mig welded 4130. Some things, however, don't change, and the quality of the finished frames – especially the chrome plated ones – is something that most of the opposition could only dream about.

Half a century on from that first ever scramble at Leighton, Brian Curtis the racer might have called it a day, but his immaculately constructed bikes will ensure that the Curtis name is kept alive for a whole new generation of scrambles fans.

Brian finished his story by telling me that his BMX bicycles are also being remade by former Curtis works rider Gary Woodhouse, and he (Brian) is involved with their construction. Not only is he brazing the frames, but his young grandson is chief test pilot for the mini bikes. So who knows, in a few years time the West Country scrambles scene might well see another Curtis out there enjoying himself.

Big thanks to Brian for reliving some wonderful trackside memories from the '60s, and for his excellent hospitality.

Early trials action. Ron on the 350cc BSA in an Alchester club event.

Ron Langston did it all on two and three wheels – trials riding, motocross, road racing – excelling at them all, and it was all done for the love of the sport.

CHAPTER 6

RON LANGSTON – GREAT ALL-ROUNDER

During the 1950s and '60s – undoubtedly the golden era of off-road motorcycle sport – there was a plethora of talented all-rounders: men like Smith, Miller, Heanes, Giles, and Jackson – not to mention several Lampkins – all capable of winning a national trial, a championship scramble, or an international six days gold medal. Undoubtedly some great competitors, but a quiet farmer from Gloucestershire was perhaps the greatest of them all. A man who was not only a works trials and scrambles rider, ISDT gold medallist, and Motocross Des Nations team member, but also a top road racer, and along with his passenger Doug Cooper was five times British trials sidecar champion. His name was Ron Langston, and in 15 years of fun-filled competition he did it all.

Forty years after he rode in his last trial Ron is now retired from farming, but he and his wife, Heather, still live in rural Gloucestershire, where I met up with him to relive some of those halcyon days.

Born in 1934, Ron was only 16 when he got his first road bike – a 350cc Ariel – but from an early age he'd watched the riders tackle the sections in the nearby Colmore Cup trial, and the thrill of this whetted his appetite enough to have a go himself.

"With the war over, motorcycle sport soon got under way again, and as some of the sections for the Colmore were only just down the road I used to ride over on my bicycle to watch. I remember once, a rider asked me to hold on to his new Triumph Trophy while he walked the section, and I decided there and then that when I was old enough I was going to get myself a trials bike. Prewar, my dad had owned and used a 1927 Ariel as his daily transport, but he had no interest in off-road sport and certainly didn't classify himself as a motorcyclist. A school friend had an old field bike which I got to ride occasionally, but I had to wait until 1951 before I got my first bike: a 350cc Ariel. I really wanted a 500, but my dad thought it was too big for me, and as it was him who was paying for it, a 350 it was.

"The previous year I'd been to the Isle of Man for the TT with my uncle and cousins, and from our vantage point at Windy Corner I just stood in awe at the speed of number one Harold Daniel, as he rushed past on his Featherbed Norton – it was a sight I'll never forget. The Ariel was OK as a road bike, but I really wanted to have a go at trials, so in the winter of '52/'53 I ordered a 350cc BSA from Stratford dealer Ralph Varden. In the early '50s a high percentage of the factory's output went for export, so I had to wait until the May of '53 before the BSA arrived. I'd decided on the Beezer simply because Norton

Ron on his way to gold in the 1956 ISDT at Garmisch in Germany.

had stopped making the 500T, and I couldn't afford a Triumph. It was terrible waiting for it, and in the meantime Ralph sorted me a ride on John Dee's 500T Norton. My first event was the Stratford 'convoy' trial, and I recall that four or five of us ended up sharing the same bike. Tackling a rocky quarry and steep climbs in the wood was all new to me, but I had a pretty good ride and amazingly when the results arrived I discovered I was the winner."

Many years later John gave him the same 500T Norton – HUE 326 – which he restored and now keeps in his collection, but by the time the next event came around in '53 the alloy-engined BSA – which would be used in both trials and scrambles – had arrived. As Ron recalled, at that time it was his only means of transport, so it was also pressed into service as an unlikely touring machine, travelling to locations as far away as Spain.

"The 1952 world champion, Cecil Sandford, lived in a village only a few miles from us in Gloucestershire, so my friend Dick Smith from Campden and I decided it would be great to go to the Spanish Grand Prix and support him. With Dick on his 500 Ariel trials bike and me on the BSA we flew the 'Silver City' from Lydd to Le Touquet, and then set off on a five-day ride through France and down into Spain. Our destination was Montjuic Park in Barcelona. In those days a lot of the roads in Spain were little more that gravel tracks, which meant that our machines were ideally suited to the rough going. During the trip Dick kept a daily diary of where we went and what we saw, which to my knowledge he's still got to this day."

Back home in Blighty, Ron was soon making a name for himself on the alloy-engined BSA, which in the days before he could afford a pick-up was fitted with a pair of 'Bobby Dodgers' and ridden to all of the events.

"It was a wonderful time for trials; the clubs had little or no trouble getting land, and there were hundreds of people competing most weekends. Most of the bikes – including my pukka trials BB32 'Alloy' BSA – were little more than modified road bikes, and we thought nothing of riding 70 or 80 miles to an event like the one at Bridgenorth, competing in the trial, and riding home again afterwards. One of my first big events was the 1954 Cotswold Cup, in which I rode with Dick Smith, John Dee, and my cousin John Righton. There were some very steep climbs, and I recall we were at the top of Ashmeads section when we heard this high-revving bike attacking it at speed. We couldn't get out of the way, so we all dived into the bushes as BSA works man John Avery hurtled up on his 500cc Gold Star for an impressive feet-up clean."

Ron was desperately keen to get himself a scrambler, and in '55 he went along to Kings in Oxford where he bought a 350cc Goldie. Sadly, after six short weeks of ownership his call-up papers arrived, so this machine was quickly replaced by something suitable for the 100-mile trip from his home in the Cotswolds to the army camp in Hampshire.

"This was also a 350cc BSA – a rigid, duplex-framed trials machine – which I bought from Ralph Varden, and one of its first events was in a class for trials bikes in a scramble at Leamington. I remember my first scramble had been on a 350cc AJS lent to me by Arthur Taylor; this was also a trials bike formerly ridden by Cecil Sandford, but we fitted a pair of knobbly tyres and it became an instant scrambler. I can't remember how I got on, but throughout my career the winning and the results weren't important – it was all about having fun.

"In June of 1955 I was called up for national service, and the BSA was used to transport me back and forth to Aldershot where I was based. It didn't have any lights, and returning to Aldershot around 5.30 one morning I was stopped by a policeman on his bicycle. 'Lighting up' was in force until 7.00am, and the policeman insisted I stopped at the roadside until the appointed hour. I wasn't really too sure what to do – I would be on a charge if I arrived late at camp – but after some head scratching I decided it was best to wait and at the stroke of seven he returned, smiled and said 'OK sonny, you can go now.'"

The two years in the army were good ones for Ron, as not only did he manage to ride in both scrambles and trials most weekends, his skill and versatility also came to the attention of Ariel's development engineer, Clive Bennett. It was the start of a friendship that lasted well over forty years, and also the opportunity of a works ride. This came about in 1956: a busy year, in which the young Langston made his debut in the Scottish six days, and also the ISDT in Germany.

"Clive had worked with Ariel competition chief Ernie Smith developing both the HT and HS models, and he suggested to me that if I wrote to Ernie there was a good chance I would get some works-supported machines. I was in the army with Eddie Dow so we got together and wrote a letter to Selly Oak. The result was a brand new HT5 trials bike – SOX 561 – which arrived just in time for the 1956 Colmore trial."

Ron took to the HT like a duck to water. Within the month he had won the trade-supported Cotswold Cup, and along with Stan Holmes and David Tye was in the Ariel team for the Scottish six days. He returned from the first of his four rides in the Highland classic with a special first-class award, and by the September he was off to Garmisch Partenkirchen with his Ariel team-mates Sammy Miller and David Tye to compete in the ISDT. He recalled that as an active serviceman he was expected to 'rough it' a bit, and after spending all day in the saddle of his Ariel there was no comfortable hotel bed to relax in.

"If I remember correctly, the bikes were taken by van while we

On GOV 130 in the Scottish six days, 1957.

"IN THE RACE ITSELF I HAD TROUBLE WITH A STICKING THROTTLE, AND WHEN THE TANK CAME LOOSE I HAD TO HOLD IT ON WITH MY KNEES"

Ron Langston on the HS at the Somerton scramble at Steart Hill.

made the trip in a VW caravanette, we stopped in Hamburg to do some testing, and then travelled on to Garmisch where the trial was based. The army didn't want us to have it too easy, so all of the service riders were billeted overnight in tents. During the trial it poured down with rain, so as you can imagine, trying to dry out soaking wet riding gear in a tent was virtually impossible. We stuck it out for three days and then one of the officers took pity on us and sorted out a hotel room, which made the world of difference."

Despite the arduous conditions, Ron returned from Germany with a well-deserved gold medal – an achievement mirrored two years later when, with national service over, he teamed up with Tim Gibbes and Gordon Blakeway at the same venue. In scrambles form the HS Ariel perhaps didn't handle as well as BSA's Gold Star, but despite its shortcomings Ron notched up numerous wins, and there were few events where the name of R J Langston didn't appear in the results. In what many regard as the 'first half' of his career covering solo trials, scrambles and the ISDT, 1958 was perhaps his most successful year. In addition to his second gold medal in the September international, he was also selected to ride for the British team in the Motocross Des Nations event in Sweden, and was narrowly beaten by British champion Dave Curtis in the prestigious Cotswold scramble in Gloucestershire.

"In the Cotswold I had a race-long dice with Dave Curtis on his works Matchless, and I was leading until the last lap, when just before the finish line I got stuck in one of those deep gullies and Dave nipped by to win. I was selected to ride in the Motocross Des Nation's team alongside the Rickman brothers, Brian Martin, John Draper, and Dave Curtis, and travelled to the event with John in his pick-up. It was blisteringly hot, and when we should have been resting they had us marching around the presentation area with all our gear on – I was knackered before we started racing. In the race itself I had trouble with a sticking throttle, and when the tank came loose I had to hold it on with my knees. The British team eventually finished second behind the Swedish line-up of Ove Lundell, Bill Nilsson, and Rolf Tibblin, but I finished a long way down the field."

Although his Motocross Des Nations debut wasn't awash in glory, there were plenty of wins for Ron and the works HS during the rest of that 1958 season, both at home and on the nearby continent. He recalled what it was like being a works-supported rider in the late '50s.

"Ariel always made sure that my bikes were in tip-top condition, and nearly every Monday after a race I took the scrambler back to the Selly Oak comp shop, where it would be rebuilt for me to pick up on the following Friday. It was very much a case of Ariel built them and I rode 'em. The one-day trials bikes would be rebuilt before a major event like the Scottish, but most of the time I fettled them myself in my workshop at home. I was riding in either a trial or scramble virtually every weekend – the bikes now transported in a Standard 10 pick-up all across the UK, and also occasionally to France and Belgium – but there was very little money in it. I was a works rider, but remember in my 'day job' I was a working farmer, so my competitive motorcycling was very much a wonderful hobby."

By now Ron was riding GOV 130 in trials, and this bike took him to another special first-class in Scotland, and also the premier in the Manville national in north Warwickshire. Later during the winter of 1958/59 he took over the works HT3 HOB 912 – a bike he now owns – but following a fall during the 1959 Experts Grand National at Rollswood, his scrambles career came to an abrupt end.

"Ariel's had made four new HS models for us works riders in 1959, and as I quickly discovered, these were a vast improvement over the old bikes. The week before the Experts Grand National I'd won on it in France, but at Rollswood I crashed heavily and ended up in a bush with the bike on top of me. I'd badly jarred the base of my spine – this a legacy of an injury from my teens when I fell through a hole in the hay loft on our farm – and I decided that I needed to put scrambling on hold while I got some treatment. It was painful, but it didn't stop me riding a bike, so in the meantime I thought to keep fit I would have a go at road racing and entered the Manx GP."

Ron already had some experience of track racing from when he'd partnered his cousin John Righton on Arthur Taylor's Velocette in the Thruxton nine-hour race, and it was John who sold him the 350 Manx Norton to ride on the island. It should be pointed out that at that time he'd never sat on – let alone raced – a pukka track machine, so before heading off to the Manx he entered a couple of short circuit races to get a feel for the bike.

"I knew Dai Pryse, a great Ariel enthusiast, and he got me a ride in his club's event in and out of the tulip beds at Aberdare Park in South Wales; it was literally a case of buying it one day and racing it the following one. A couple of weeks later I rode at Brands Hatch, and then I was off to the Isle of Man for what was only my third proper race."

To say that Ron's Manx debut was sensational is an understatement. He was soon on the pace in practice, impressing the crowds with his style and speed, and in the race eventually finished an astounding second behind Peter Middleton on his 350cc Norton. Ernie Earles also lent him a 500, but as a newcomer the organisers wouldn't allow him to ride it, so he had to wait until 1960 before he made his 500cc debut on a G50 Matchless prepared by Geoff Monty. In fact, 1960 was a memorable year for Ron: not only did he ride the pair of Monty-prepared bikes to a fine double in the Southern 100, he also partnered Don Chapman on a 6500cc AJS to victory in the Thruxton 500 miler, and in August tied the knot with his girlfriend, Heather. The newlyweds chose the Manx over a honeymoon, but for Ron the races were disappointing ones, riddled with machine failures, and shortly after returning home he received the news that Ariel was closing its competition department and he was looking for another ride.

"Ariel took the bikes back and sold them; after riding for them for many years I thought that perhaps we could have bought them at a fair price, but they wanted a lot for them and I had to content myself with an HS scrambler. I had an offer from DOT, and then Hugh Viney lent me a 350cc Matchless – which was undoubtedly a lovely bike – but I just couldn't ride it like the Ariel, and I let him have it back. I'd enjoyed every minute of my trials riding career, but decided it was time to retire from solos and have a go at sidecar trials instead."

The first outfit – based around the HS scrambler he'd bought from Ariel – was soon taking shape, although at that time Ron could have little imagined that it was the start of another memorable part of his trials career – one that would see him and his passenger Doug Cooper scoop five British Championship titles and numerous premier awards in important nationals the length and breadth of the country.

"Helped by Ken Turner, I made up a sidecar and got the local blacksmith in Campden to weld it to the frame of the detuned HS scrambler. I can't remember where I first rode it, but I tried out a couple of different passengers before I teamed up with Doug Cooper. Doug called round one day and I mentioned that I was looking for a

Motocross Des Nations in Sweden, 1958.

ISDT action from Garmisch in 1958, with Ron on his way to a gold medal.

Winning the Thruxton 500-miler on the AJS twin, June 1960.

passenger. His instant reply was 'I'd like that job,' so he jumped in and we hit it off straight away. He'd had quite a lot of experience of riding a solo in trials, and in the sidecar he was fantastic. In trials the passenger needs to keep as much weight as possible on the back wheel of the bike, and just enough on the sidecar to hold it down, and Doug was marvellous at doing that. It seemed like he could read my mind and had an instinct for when we were about to break traction; it didn't matter how fast or slow we were going, he was always there in the right place at the right time."

In national trials during the '60s there was a plethora of sidecar talent, and every winter weekend Ron was doing battle with the likes of Ken and Des Kendall, Alan Morewood, Alec Wright, and Arthur and Lyn Pulman, while the summer months saw him dicing with some of the world's best road racers. During three action-packed seasons – 1960, '61 and '62 – he not only competed in his favourite Isle of Man TT, where on Geoff Monty's very quick G50 Matchless he finished 5th in the '61 Senior, but also rode twice in the Italian, Ulster and Belgian GPs, the latter at Spa, where in '61 he was cruelly robbed of a podium at the last corner.

"Having the farm to run I always considered myself to be a 'holiday racer,' and was flattered when the organisers wrote to me and asked me to ride in the Belgian GP. Geoff Monty's G50 wasn't available, so he contacted Jack Williams at AMC and arranged for me to have a works bike, which I would pick up from the factory on my way to the ferry. I arrived at the Plumstead factory very early in the morning, and couldn't even find the night watchman; but what I did find was the works Matchless stood outside in the road waiting to be collected. I assumed it was for me, so I loaded it up and drove off to Spa. After about two laps in the race the nut holding the clutch in position came loose, which meant I had to ride the whole race making clutchless changes. This was OK, other than at the very slow La Source hairpin, where I couldn't get it on the megaphone quickly enough, and on the last lap Mike Duff slipped by and I was beaten into fourth place, which was extremely frustrating."

There were plenty of other close finishes for the flying Gloucestershire farmer during the next couple of seasons. The first time I saw him racing was in the '62 Thruxton 500, where he shared a 650ss Norton with journalist Bruce Main-Smith. With the skills they'd developed from riding their Ariel trials outfit, Ron and Doug also tried their hand at circuit racing on an unusual four-cylinder 500cc machine, which unfortunately blew up on its debut in a big way.

"We had the opportunity to try out a road-racing sidecar, which was powered by an Ariel four-cylinder engine; not a square four, but two leader two-stroke engines joined together. We went to Snetterton in May '62 and then took it to the island for the TT, but sadly we only got as far as the Islander when a rod broke and we coasted to a stop, leaving a trail of assorted crank case and con rod bits scattered across the road."

It was the pair's first and only outing on a road-racing sidecar, and from the winter of '62/'63 onwards they concentrated all their efforts on sidecar trials – although as Ron told me, this was not without incident or injury.

"We went everywhere, from the Red Rose in the north, to the West of England in the south, but we didn't keep any records of what we did – we simply rode because we enjoyed it. We remained remarkably free from injuries, but I do remember one southern Experts where there was a long muddy climb up a ditch. I was wringing the neck of the Ariel in third, and with Doug hanging out the side I was practically in the sidecar, when suddenly it started to go higher and higher until I couldn't hold it and we went straight though a hedge. We finished the trial, but I later discovered I'd broken my wrist, which was then in plaster for the next thirteen weeks."

Other than the inevitable cuts and bruises, Doug remained remarkably free of injury in the chair. However, in 1965 he broke his arm at work, and with the Colmore coming up Ron needed a new crewman. After clearing it with the lad's father he recruited a young neighbour, 16-year-old Rusty Hart, and in an inspired ride they won the trial, the delighted Rusty receiving the winner's cup from Ron in recognition of his superb efforts. Rusty, Roman Ziel, and Fred Hewitt also crewed until Doug was fit again, and Aubrey Smith partnered Ron once in the Manx two-day trial; but the pairing of Langston and Cooper was a formidable one, and for two or three seasons was virtually unbeatable. During that time they had only two Ariel outfits: the first (677 ADD) served them up until 1967, while the second (the home built LDF 53E) saw them through to the southern Experts, their final British Championship title, and their retirement in 1968.

For those lucky enough to have witnessed Ron Langston in action, the memories of the crisp bark of his Ariel at a full head of steam, and the look of determination etched in every sinew of his face, will live forever. Not only were we lucky enough to have seen one of motorcycling's greatest all-rounders, but also a truly modest man who did it all for the best reasons: not fame or money, but love and enjoyment of the sport. I'll leave the last words to him:

"Nothing but good has come out of trials riding and motorcycling for me; I've had a wonderful time, made some great friends, and enjoyed every minute of it."

Big thanks to Ron and Heather for all their help and hospitality, and for reliving some wonderful memories from the golden days of motorcycle sport.

Ron and Doug Cooper in the DK Mansell trophy trial.

Ron (6) on the 500cc Norton leads Franta Stasny's 385cc Jawa.

Ron and Doug Cooper in the Pierce Simon trial, 3 November 1964.

A long way up on the 500cc Gold Star.

During the glory days of British scrambling, Terry Cox was often at the sharp end of the field, nearly always riding a big, booming four-stroke.

CHAPTER 7

TERRY COX - FOUR-STROKE FAN

From an early age, the Cox family paddock in the Somerset village of Keinton Mandeville was both a playground and motorcycle test field to the young Terry Cox. A Douglas twin and an old Ivy were two of the many bikes slid around in great style by the boy who, in the 1960s, would become one of the West Country's leading scrambles stars, and a future south western centre champion

I first saw Terry racing on the steep slopes of the Mendips in 1961. On that memorable day – my first scramble – the short, tigerish rider displaying number 50 was locked in a start-to-finish duel with the Rickman and Sharp brothers, and Ivor England; a thrilling race that saw the lead change hands several times before the younger Rickman got ahead to win from Triss Sharp, with Cox a close third. For scrambles fans they were truly memorable days, and nearly half a century later I was lucky enough to visit Terry and his wife, Jean, at their west Somerset home. We relived that day at Westbury-sub-Mendip, the tricky hillside venue where, in 1955, the young Cox had also made his race debut, coming to the line on a 350cc Triumph – a bike that, as he told me, was sadly short of power.

"I'd been tearing around dad's paddock on his old bikes when I was spotted by a chap called Phil Deny. Phil would pass by on his way to the nearby pub, and often stop and watch me tearing around. I guess that he must have been impressed, because one day out of the blue he asked if he could sponsor me on a scrambles bike. As you can imagine I didn't need to be asked twice, and soon after getting the Triumph I entered my first event at Westbury-sub-Mendip. We took the bike to the scramble on a home-built trailer behind dad's V8 Ford Pilot, and in my first race I was going pretty well, but sadly the Triumph was suffering from a serious lack of power. I had to push it up the steep back hill, and in an effort to catch the leaders I went too fast and crashed, breaking my wrist in the process."

On leaving school Terry got an apprenticeship as a mechanic with Vincent's in Yeovil – a company where he would work for the next fifteen years. Along with his friend, Des Brown, he began experimenting with ways of improving the little Triumph's power output.

"Des and I decided to put the Triumph on dope, which did a lot to improve the power, but unfortunately it kept blowing up. At that time, Garth Jotcham – the editor of the south western centre's *Gazette* – had a shop in nearby Burnham on Sea, so he was a good source for spares and advice. All of the engine blow ups, however, didn't please the sponsor too much, but soon I was lucky enough to buy an ex-Jim Alves Gold Star engine, and started to get a bit of success on it."

The result of a very heavy landing, with the Goldie's rear wheel looking very secondhand.

"I RACED VIRTUALLY EVERY WEEKEND FOR TWENTY YEARS, AND I CAN NEVER THANK ALL THE FRIENDS WHO HELPED AND SUPPORTED ME DURING THAT TIME ENOUGH"

After a couple of seasons and several wins under his belt, Terry became an established expert in the south western centre, and began to be noticed. Among those taking notes were Ralph Venables, who, after reporting that "a diminutive new boy from Somerton" had won the 1958 Dorset Grand National, prophesied that he was destined for a long and successful career. In fact 1958, was turning out to be a very good year for Terry, as not only did he win the Dorset Grand National, he also beat Paul Jarman and the up-and-coming Dave Bickers into third place at the Broadhembury club's unlimited final.

The same year also gave him what he described as his "biggest break."

"I'd just bought a year-old Goldie from Ivor England, and was at the long Higher Farm Wick course at Glastonbury when someone tapped me on the shoulder: it turned out to be Harold Wakefield. I believe Harold's family were the Wakefield oil people, and he had two great passions in his life: golf and motorcycle scrambling. Later in the '60s he would go on to support many southern county riders, but at that time was just sponsoring the Rickman brothers, and asked me if he could buy me a new bike. In his own quiet way Harold turned out to be very generous with his sponsorship, and I ended up with two beautiful brand new DBD 34 BSAs and an Austin A55 pick-up truck."

It would be the start of a long association between the two, and later Terry would ride an ex-Triss Sharp 500cc Triumph, a 250cc Greeves, and both a Triumph and Bultaco-engined Metisse, all supplied by Wakefield. On the booming four-strokes the sight of Cox in full flight was an impressive sight, although his outings on two-strokes were not so successful.

"Early on in my career I had a one-off ride on an ex-John Clayton 250cc Francis Barnett, and then rode the Greeves for a few weeks, and although I won a race at Crediton I just couldn't get on with two-strokes. After riding 380lb of Gold Star it felt like I was racing on a push bike."

Terry didn't just become a top class scrambler. He also was a useful trials rider, the highlight of which came about in the winter of 1959. By then he'd progressed from a James Commando to a 500T Norton, and in a muddy West of England trial he rode superbly, losing only 11 marks, and in doing so beat several of the established feet up stars, including local west country star Jim Alves. He was proving to be both a good trials and scrambles rider, but in fact his first love had been road racing, and if it hadn't been for parental opposition he could have become a tarmac racer.

"I loved going fast on the road, and owned a racing Manx Norton which was taxed and registered. It had no kick start so I had to bump start it everywhere, but it went like an absolute rocket and on a good day I could get from our home in Keinton Mandeville down the Fosse Way to my work in Yeovil in seven minutes. I wanted to go road racing on it but my dad didn't approve, so I stuck with scrambles and trials, although later in my career I rode my Triumph Metisse in a couple of special speedway events organised for scrambles bikes. It was good fun and it also paid pretty well; in fact, I've still got the programme showing that in the final prize money was £10 for first, down to 10 shillings for 6th place."

For those of us who followed scrambles in the '60s Terry was usually seen wearing number 50, on his bikes and I asked him how this came about.

"There was no particular reason, but when I entered my first race I opted on number 50 and decided to stick with it. In those days you kept your racing number for a season and only needed to change it if you raced in another centre."

Terry was certainly a south western star, representing both his home town Somerton and the centre in team events. In fact, he raced in no fewer than 15 inter-centre events, mostly for the south western team, although as he lived in the area bordering two centres he also raced on a couple of occasions for Wessex.

In 1960 he also won the hand of his sweetheart Jean – the sister of fellow scrambler Brian Trott – and she told me how they had first met, about their first eventful date, and the day of their wedding: a day when her husband-to-be turned up looking like he'd been in a fight.

"I first met Terry at Ye Old Pop Inn at Tatworth after a scramble. I asked him how he'd got on racing that day and he said "not too bad" – I later learnt he'd won all his races. He asked me out for a date at Bridgwater fair, but on the way there we skidded and he ended up rolling his Austin 10, thankfully without serious injury. We married in 1960, but the weekend before the wedding he'd come off at Haddon hill and turned up at the church with five stitches in a gash across his face."

Terry added with a grin "I've still got the scars."

"Worse was to follow as four days later there was an important race so our honeymoon was put on hold; sadly Terry crashed and broke his leg, which was not the perfect wedding present."

Assisted by Jean and his team of friends, and helpers Dezzy Brown, Ashley Middleton, John Purchase, and his brother Michael Cox, Terry was in action virtually every weekend, often in his home south western centre. Although, as he told me, in the early '60s he started to look further afield, managing to get some rides in the lucrative continental meetings.

"Trying to get a break to race on the continent was not easy, but I got a few organisers addresses from Eric Cheney and then some more from Arthur Harris. On his home-built, stubby looking Triumph specials Arthur raced almost exclusively in France, and was known to all his friends as 'Continental Joe.' Along with my friend Norman Alan – who used to work for Ken Heanes in Fleet – we got some entries accepted, and after a while became well accepted by the organisers and the large enthusiastic French crowds. I usually got around £100 start money – which was a lot more than I was picking up at the garage – but as you can imagine, a weekend spent travelling the length of France, racing, and then getting back home for work on Monday morning was extremely tiring. For about three seasons I raced regularly on the continent and had some good rides with a few seconds and thirds, but my only win came in a scramble near Lyon in 1963, something I was very chuffed about."

Both at home and abroad, the booming four-stroke and its all-action rider were great favourites with the crowds – although just getting the bike to the start line often demanded some hard work from his team of helpers.

"I raced virtually every weekend – often four races per meeting – for twenty years, and I can never thank all the friends who helped and supported me during that time enough. Dezzy Brown who assisted me in preparing the bikes, often working through the night; Ashley Middleton who did a lot of the mechanical repairs; John Purchase, mechanic at the meetings; and my brother Michael, a great supporter and helper."

Typical Terry Cox racing style on the big Gold Star, at an event in west Somerset in the late 1950s.

A determined Terry on his championship-winning Triumph Metisse.

Michael in fact shared the same name as a '60s pop star, and was once introduced by Badger Goss as the very same man; the crowd's request for a song turned down because "I'm under contract to Decca."

Although he was a naturally talented rider, off the race track Terry enjoyed a drink or two, and he revealed that when racing at the Buckfastleigh meetings at Dean Prior in Devon, he sometimes came to the start line with a hangover.

"When we were racing at Dean Prior I usually travelled down on the Saturday to have a bed and breakfast at the Waterman's Arms in Buckfastleigh. Incidentally, B&B for the three of us cost £3 7s 6d and I've still got the invoice. The pub – which served a good pint – was run by Dot and George Higsdon, and was a popular Saturday night haunt for the riders before the racing on the Sunday. After official closing time George would lock the door, and Pete Tizzard and I would keep him company until the early hours of Sunday morning. I remember once we got to bed at 4am just as the postman dropped by to have an early morning pint on his way to collect the mail. I had quite a hangover as I came to the line the next day, but in the main race I was dicing for the lead with Gerald Winsor when we came up to lap George. George was a junior rider and he'd borrowed my spare bike, but as we overtook him he moved over and in doing so accidentally hit Gerald off, and I won the race. Gerald was never entirely convinced it was not a 'put up job,' although we did share a laugh about it later on."

During the early '60s the line-up of Cox, the Jarman brothers, and John Tribble was almost unbeatable in the centre team events, and such was their dominance that rivals complained they should be banned for a season to give someone else a chance at the trophy. In the south western championships Cox had several times finished close runner-up, but it took a change of machine for him to scoop his first title.

Although still fast, the ex-Sharp Triumph had – despite Terry's skill – lost its handling edge, but thanks to Harold Wakefield the potent twin was rehoused in a brand new Rickman Metisse rolling chassis, on which Terry won the first of his two championship titles. On his home ground, the combination of Cox and the Metisse was an almost unbeatable one, and on one of his favourite tracks at Newton St Cyres in Devon he recorded a remarkable 14 wins from 16 starts – stunning performances that earned him selection for the southern team in the annual tussle against the north. On that day he finished in a creditable mid-table position, but was soon back to his best to win the first Yeo Vale Bass-Charrington trophy, the Somerset Grand National, and the Avalon Trophy at Glastonbury.

He also enjoyed racing at Biggin Hill in Kent, a circuit that suited his full bore broad sliding style, especially when wet and muddy. After riding the Metisse to a win he was approached by a speedway promoter.

"The chap was one of the promoters from Bristol speedway, who approached me and asked if I was interested in giving cinder racing a go; of course I'd already raced a few times in the special scrambles bike races, but although it was tempting I decided to stick to scrambling and trials."

In one of his scrambles reports Ralph Venables described Terry as a 'master of the mud,' but sometimes his over exuberance led to a crash and a trip to the Saint Johns ambulance tent. He laughed as he recalled that several times he was so battered and bruised he was unable to drive his van home from the meeting.

For a while he raced a BSA Victor Metisse, and although he was often sidelined with problems with the Weslake conversion his performances didn't go unnoticed by Small Heath's Brian Martin.

"Brian supplied me with an ex-works B50, and with its Reynolds frame and lightweight electron cases it was a super bike to ride. On the race tracks the two-strokes were starting to take the upper hand, and although I wasn't an official 'works' rider Brian Martin looked after me really well and regularly had the bike back to the factory for a new big end and an engine overhaul."

On the BSA the name of Terry Cox was spread to a bigger audience with some stirring appearances in the TV *Grandstand* trophy, where he was regularly referred to by Murray Walker as "one of the last four-stroke riders."

With the collapse of BSA he soon got a new ride on one of Alan Clews' CCMs – a bike he bought in 1973, and one he would race until he retired two years later. By now he was past his best, but as he told me, the day he hung up his leathers was not the end of his involvement with scrambling, or with the CCM.

"I'd raced every weekend for close on twenty years, and as I was then busy running my own garage business I decided to call it a day. I thought that might be the end of my days working on scrambles bikes, but I was then asked by Alan Clews if I would like to help out as mechanic to John Banks and Bob Wright in some of the World Championship rounds."

This was a job Terry did for the next two seasons, although it was an incident away from the track he remembers best.

"We were in Austria, and met a chap called Count Otto Herberstein – a very wealthy man who had a castle on a huge estate. He owned several bikes, including an ex-works BSA, and had his own personal scrambles track, which Puch used to test their bikes on. He wined and dined the riders superbly, but after leaving the castle the next day we had an accident in the van, which sent poor old Bob Wright through the windscreen. Fortunately, this was without serious injury, but understandably Alan Clews was not very pleased with the damage to the van, and it was a very cold drive back to England.

"I kept the CCM in my garage, and when classic scrambling started my son-in-law Martin Perrett raced it for me; in fact, he's done pretty well on it and is still racing it today."

Like the great days from the '50s and '60s when Terry's mum and dad followed their son all over the country, the Cox clan of Terry, Jean, daughter Elaine, and her children, Brad and Alanna, are at most of today's classic events, watching and cheering-on Martin and the booming CCM. The name of Terry Cox discreetly displayed on the bike's side panel is a fitting reminder of one of the West Country's most popular and successful scramblers from a golden era.

Many thanks to Terry and Jean for all of their time and hospitality in compiling this profile.

On the 500cc Triumph Metisse that Terry raced so successfully during the mid-'60s.

Plenty of poise and style on the works BSA (location unknown).

Derek and Don receiving their cups at a very early age.

The Rickman brothers took on and beat the world on their home brewed machine, the Metisse: a mongrel with a pedigree.

CHAPTER 8

DEREK AND DON RICKMAN

The period of the late '50s and early '60s was undoubtedly a golden era for scrambling, with a plethora of top notch British stars all capable of taking on and beating the best in the world. Two of the best were undoubtedly the brothers Derek and Don Rickman from New Milton in Hampshire. A pair of highly talented men, who were not only world class riders, but also the designers and manufacturers of the machine that revolutionised off-road sport: the Metisse.

Forty years have now elapsed since Derek and Don hung up their racing leathers, but the Metisse – the name first conjured up in Harold Wakefield's front room in the summer of 1959 – is still going strong. Whenever in the world of pre-'65 scrambling a booming exhaust note can be heard, it's a safe bet the engine will be housed in an exquisitely crafted nickel frame with the evocative name of Metisse on the petrol tank.

That the Rickmans became reluctant manufacturers in the 1960s is little known – this after all of the industry's big players had declined the brothers' offer to build the race-winning frames – but it's just one of many interesting stories that I discovered when I journeyed to New Milton to meet up with Derek and Don, the dashing duo who, in the early '60s, were two of my boyhood heroes.

For me they were carefree days, magical Sundays spent travelling with my big brother Rod in his A40 van to the Wessex and southern centre circuits of Higher Farm Wick, Farleigh Castle, Leighton, Matcham's Park, and Giant's Head. Long, sweeping courses that reverberated to the booming beat of crackling exhaust pipes, where the aroma of the burnt Castrol R hung like an invisible veil in the summer sun. Courses well known to the Rickman brothers.

That Derek and Don became racing motorcyclists was hardly surprising. Before the war, their father, Ernie, was an accomplished cinder star for the Southampton speedway team, and as little more than toddlers the brothers would accompany their mother, Marjorie, to watch him in action. They grew up with the sound and smells of flying cinders and roaring JAP speedway engines filling their senses, and by the time they were aged ten and eight Ernie had built them a couple of stripped-down Austin sevens, which they raced around the field at the back of his garage. It wasn't long, however, before their attentions turned to two wheels, and with a degree of resourcefulness they fitted a side-valve Triumph P engine into one of their father's old speedway frames. This was the first 'Rickman,' and on it they not only had a lot of fun sliding it around the field, but learnt much about throttle control

Derek on a BSA Gold Star in the 1950s.

"THEIR RAW TALENT WAS THERE FOR ALL TO SEE, AND THEN LADY LUCK CAME THEIR WAY WITH SOME GENEROUS SPONSORSHIP FROM HAROLD WAKEFIELD"

Derek riding the first Metisse at Aldmouth near Reading.

and balance that would hold them in such good stead in later years. It was a good grounding, and Derek told me a little about those early years and how his competition career got under way in 1949.

"Dad ran a business repairing and servicing cars, but motorcycles were his first love, and up to the outbreak of the Second World War in 1939 he rode for the Southampton Saints speedway team. I think I must have been about three or four when I went to watch my first race, but of course this was all interrupted by the war. When competition restarted he decided to have a go at trials and bought himself a BSA B32, but sadly at the age of 45 he suffered a stroke and died before he could ride it. At that time I was still a boarder at the Kings School at Bruton where there was plenty of time for extra-curricula activities like riding motorcycles across the playing fields. We persuaded mum not to sell the BSA and on it Don and I put in countless hours riding around the nearby woods and fields. We got pretty good at negotiating all sorts of rough and slippery ground, and after we'd gone along to spectate at a couple of XHG Tigers scrambles we decided to have a go ourselves. In those days there was no schoolboy sport, so frustratingly I had to wait until I was sixteen before I could get my competition licence and ride competitively."

It was soon obvious that the hours spent riding the BSA had been well spent, as Derek scooped the novice award in his first event – the Tiger Ash trial at nearby Christchurch – and later the same year won the novice race at the Ringwood club scramble at Matcham's Park.

Born in 1935, younger brother Don had to wait until 1951 before he could also start his competition career, but from his debut ride at East Meon he immediately looked a natural, and before his first season was out he'd joined his elder brother in the Experts. By 1952, the Rickmans were mounted on a pair of BSA Gold Stars, and were the rising stars of the southern centre. Their raw talent was there for all to see, and then lady luck came their way with some generous sponsorship from Harold Wakefield.

"After dad died, our mum, Marjorie, took over the running of the garage business, and we persuaded her to buy us a couple of BSA scramblers. We were starting to get a few wins under our belts, and after a good day at Bulbarrow Hill in Dorset she was approached by Harold Wakefield, who asked her if he could sponsor us. He was a shy reserved man who didn't push himself forward, but he was extremely generous, and with some decent bikes – a pair of new Gold Stars from Huxham's – we were soon on our way."

Before the war, Harold Wakefield – who the brothers later learnt was part of the Wakefield oil concern – had sponsored his cousin Johnny racing in car GPs, but sadly the man who had the potential to be a future world champion was killed in the war, and when peace returned Harold turned his attentions to two wheels. On the Wakefield-sponsored Goldies Don and Derek were soon starting to make people notice the Rickman name, and there were countless races when either 73 DE or 74 DJ was first past the flag. At the age of 19, Derek entered the 1952 British Grand Prix held on the demanding 2.5-mile long circuit at Nympsfield in Gloucestershire – the first to be held in the UK – and after a race-long duel with Belgian Victor Leloup and America's Bud Ekins he brought his Goldie home to a fine third place, behind Brian Stonebridge and Phil Nex. It was an auspicious start to his international career, but not to be outdone, a month later his 17-year-old brother finished sixth in the unlimited final of the southern centre championship meeting at Beenham Park. Derek's scintillating form saw him selected for the southern team in the annual race against the north near Bury, but getting to the northern venue was quite a challenge. There were no fancy race transporters, and in the pre-motorway days the long journey was made with the front wheel of the BSA removed and the bike towed to the start, with the forks tied to the back bumper of a Triumph Gloria car.

The brothers were also spreading their wings further afield. Derek told me about one of his early trips to France in 1952, which he made with his friend and rival Triss Sharp.

"I made my first trip to the continent to Holland in 1951, where I met the organisers of the big scramble held at the old chalk pits at Montrieul in the suburbs of Paris. Keen to have some British riders they invited me over to race the following year, so Triss and I took our bikes on the boat train from Weymouth to Paris. There we were met by Mr Charliet who ran the BSA agency in Paris, but sadly his van wasn't big enough to carry our two bikes so with no tax or insurance our only option was to ride the unsilenced bikes through the centre of the French capital to the track. France was still recovering from the aftermath of the war and the meeting attracted thousands of spectators who were keen to see us all negotiate a steep 20 foot drop known as 'Le Grand Decent.' The organisers paid us some decent start money, and in the main race I had a good ride and managed to finish in the top six. It was all extremely exciting stuff."

In his day job Derek had begun work as an apprentice at Thorneycroft's Lorries. The skills he learnt on the drawing boards would hold him in good stead when later he and Don (who had joined Westover garages in nearby Bournemouth) designed the first Metisse frame. However, their first love was racing motorcycles, and although work had to be put on hold for two years when Derek was called up for national service, it did little to hinder his burgeoning scrambling career. Based at RAF Sopley – just a few miles from Matcham's Park – meant he could ride virtually every weekend in scrambles or wintertime trials, but an injury prevented him from competing in the '53 British GP. Still only 17, Don was left to carry the Rickman flag, and in a race eventually won by Brian Stonebridge he did so in dashing style, bringing the Goldie home in fourth place against some of the best riders in the world.

The wins were coming thick and fast on the Wakefield-sponsored Gold Stars, but the industry's big three of BSA, Triumph and AMC were slow to sign the two southern centre stars, and as Don explained, their first works ride came from a slightly unlikely source.

"Although Royal Enfield made some decent one and six day trials bikes, they didn't have much of a track record with their scramblers, and after testing they offered us a couple of factory bikes. Prior to that none of the factories had shown any interest in us, but less than two hours after we'd signed for Enfield, Hugh Viney contacted us and invited us to ride for AMC, which of course we had to refuse.

"The engines in the Enfields were actually pretty good, and in the first trade-supported meeting of the '55 season Derek and I managed to finish first and second in the Hants Grand National at Matchams. We picked up a few more wins in other open-to-centre events, but when ridden hard in the national and international races the frames constantly broke, and the whole suspension system wasn't up to the task. We used to send the bikes back to Redditch every week on the train to be repaired, and after a while we got a call from Enfield asking us if we could ride every other weekend so they could have more time to repair them!"

Don riding a prototype Triumph Metisse.

"WE DIDN'T TAKE OUR SOCKS OFF FOR THREE DAYS, AND IT WAS ALL PRETTY EXHAUSTING"

Beenham Championship, 1962. D J Rickman on the prototype petite Metisse with 196cc Bultaco engine.

Don and Derek rode the Enfields for two seasons before going back to Gold Stars, which – although more ruggedly built than the Redditch singles – were heavy bikes, and hard pushed to match the sweet handling Swedish Monark and Lito machines they encountered in the international races. It was here that the first seeds of building their own frames were planted, but while these germinated, Don had his first outing on a factory two-stroke Dot: a bike that was fast but frail.

"At that time Dot scramblers were powered by Villiers singles, but they were also experimenting with an RCA twin-engined bike. When it was going it was quite fast and I won the Lancs Grand National and finished second on it in the 250cc Cotswold, but the engine was a nightmare as it had a tendency to overheat and would seize up for a pastime. Some years later Derry Preston-Cobb persuaded me to try a Greeves, but although it suited Stonebridge and Bickers I couldn't get on with it; a single meeting at Winchester was my one and only outing on the Thundersly two-strokes."

The back end of the 1956 season had seen Derek mounted on an AJS as a substitute for the wrecked Enfield, and the following season the brothers were once again back on the old faithful BSA Gold Stars. For the older Rickman, 1957 was a glorious season that culminated in his selection in the victorious British Motocross Des Nations team, but for Don it was one of mixed fortunes. Things started well with a second behind Les Archer at the southern Scott and a win in the junior race at the Hants Grand National, but shortly after being called up for national service he crashed at the Cotswold and badly broke his wrist. This injury kept him out of the saddle for the rest of the year, and it also saw his discharge from the army. "I did two years and Don did two weeks," Derek recalled with a wry laugh!

Marjorie Rickman had run the family garage business since her husband's death, but it was not directly related to the brothers' sporting prowess, so with motorcycle sales booming the decision was made to sell the garage and open a bike shop in New Milton. The new business – which fronted a purpose-built workshop – opened its doors in July 1958, and it would be from here that the first Metisse would appear twelve months later.

MkIII frames in production, early 1960s. Eddie Burroughs and Pete Pykett are in the background.

The production Gold Star was a big heavy beast, and its handling shortcomings were there for all to see in the '58 Motocross Des Nations, which was dominated by the Swedes on their lightweight Crescent and Monark machines. British riders like Les Archer, Eric Cheney, and Arthur Harris had spent much of their careers racing on the continent, and had shown that to be competitive a sweet handling 'special' was the way forward. Derek and Don were quick to take up the challenge, and in great secrecy during the long winter of 1958/59, they turned their ideas into metal. Without any advance publicity the bike – which was finished only days before – was wheeled out for its public debut at Bulbarrow Hill in March 1959. It was captured on film by Gordon Francis, and after watching Derek dominate the Experts and solo star races – Don was sidelined by flu – he reported the machine as being "a terrifically potent Triumph engine special."

At that time the bike was very much a TriBSA, but the name of Metisse would soon follow. Derek told me how the bike and its name came about.

"In its day the Gold Star was a decent machine, but during a hard race the frame and the rear swinging arm would bend and twist, which meant that the wheels would be running out of line and the chain would be very slack. Don and I decided that the only way forward was to make a bike incorporating the best which was available, plus some ideas of our own. Through working at Thorneycroft Lorries I had some experience of engineering drawings, so we set up a drawing board in the backroom and set to. Our first bikes were based around a pre-unit Triumph twin engine housed in a strengthened and modified Gold Star frame, and from the outset we were acutely aware of the basic need for the wheels to follow each other in a constant straight line. We strengthened the steering head, and to save weight we dispensed with the oil tank and carried the oil in the frame tubes, which allowed the engine to run much cooler than with a conventional oil tank.

"After the race at Bulbarrow we stopped off for the customary cup of tea at Harold Wakefield's house in Ferndown, and we were asked what we were going to call our new machine. As it was a bike which had a Triumph engine in a BSA frame, Norton forks, BSA gearbox clutch and wheels, we suggested it was very much a mongrel, and although apt we felt it was associated too much with the dog world. With that a French dictionary was produced and the name of Metis – Metisse in its female form – came to light, and from that day onwards our mongrel had a pedigree! I guess from the time we did the first drawings to the day the MkI was ready to race took about two years."

Derek also recalled that the now distinctive tank logo came courtesy of a local retired sign writer, who designed and hand-painted it in the garage at the back of his house!

Within three weeks a second machine was finished for Don to ride, and he romped to victory in the allcomers race in the March Hare. In his report, Neville Goss – later to become a Rickman employee – used the name 'Metisse' for the first time in the results, and people started to sit up and take notice of the bike with the unforgettable name.

After wins in the important Sunbeam point-to-point and Wessex national, May saw the Metisse make its overseas debut in France, quickly followed the next month by its first appearance in a Grand Prix. Under the Italian sun at Imola both brothers were in terrific form, and at the end of a gruelling day's racing – won overall by Sten Lundin –

Don following Derek at an early 1960s Tweseldown race near Aldershot.

Don Rickman on his way to win the final of a televised trophy event, Beaulieu 1964.

Derek was second and Don third, while the works BSAs languished in sixth, seventh and ninth places. A week later there were two more impressive second places in the West German Grand Prix, but unlike the Small Heath men who were paid to race their works bikes, the Rickmans had a business to run, and Don recalled there was precious time to draw breath or enjoy the sights on their travels.

"A typical Easter would see us racing in the Hants Grand National on the Friday, work on Saturday morning, then home to prepare the bikes, before loading the pick-up and heading off to Belgium for a race on Sunday. Sunday night we would sleep in the pick-up and do a meeting in France on the Monday, before catching the late night ferry back to Dover. We then had the long drive back to Hampshire for work on Tuesday morning. We didn't take our socks off for three days, and it was all pretty exhausting."

Wins for both DE and DJ Rickman came by the score during that '58 season, but Don's enduring memory of a fantastic year is his victory in annual Motocross Des Nations team race. Derek was sidelined through injury, but in only his second ride for the national side the younger Rickman was in superb form. At the end of a hard dusty day's racing he emerged overall winner, and with excellent back-up from Jeff Smith (fifth) and John Draper (sixth) the British beat the much-fancied Swedes for the team prize. Barely six months after it had been first raced, the Metisse had taken on and beaten the best in the world.

The MkI's first season was rounded off in fine style when Don led the southern team to victory in the inter-centre team event, but not content to sit on their laurels, the brothers were already planning its next incarnation. The MkII made its debut at the 1960 Hants Grand National, and with Derek aboard it finished fourth behind Jeff Smith, Don on the MkI, and John Burton's Gold Star. A crowd soon gathered round the new Metisse, and although still basically a TriBSA it was visually a very different machine to the MkI. Ever conscious of the need to have an efficient air filter to minimise engine wear – mechanic 'Tiny' Camfield was forever fitting new barrels and pistons on the MkI – this had been addressed by fitting an oil air filter similar to the ones used on trucks, and also a paper one, mounted within a lightweight GRP moulding. To make the bike as light as possible, the Rickmans had turned to Doug Mitchenall at Avon Fairings (in later years Doug would join the Rickman workforce) to make a tail unit out of glass reinforced plastic, and this distinctive shape would be the hallmark of all future Metisse bodywork. The net result of the new air filter was that the engine went the entire season without being stripped.

The next two seasons were memorable ones, with both Derek and Don notching up numerous wins on the crisp sounding and sweet handling Metisse, but they were ever aware that they couldn't be complacent and were always looking to the future. A MkII with leading link forks – a weight saving of 10lb over a conventional set of telescopics – carried Don to victory at a TV scramble at Beaulieu, but although popular with the thousands of armchair viewers, these wintertime mud-baths found little favour with the Rickmans, who considered scrambling to be a summer sport.

There was a business to run and a new frame to design and build, but the brothers were always looking to broaden their horizons, and the winter of 1960 heralded the start of a long and successful association with Bultaco. Don takes up the story:

"Up until 1960 Bultaco had concentrated all of their production on road and road racing machines, but they were interested into breaking into off-road sport, so they contacted the ACU in London for ways and means of developing that aim. Motocross supremo Harold Taylor recommended us to Francisco Bulto and a few weeks later Derek and I were bound for Barcelona. The first week we spent converting and tuning ten new Bultacos into scrambles trim, and we then had another week putting them and a group of would-be Spanish motocrossers through some rigorous testing and training."

At the end of the second week Don and the newly finished 175cc Bultaco came to the start line for the first ever Barcelona Grand Prix, and in front of a huge crowd – estimated at 30-40,000 – gave the little two-stroke a glorious debut as he ran out overall winner ahead of fellow Brits Ian Horsell, Mike Jackson, Triss Sharp, and Dave Curtis. The Spanish crowd went wild, and Francisco Bulto was understandably delighted.

There was no doubt that the Spanish machine had a lot of potential, and the Rickmans immediately arranged for it to be shipped back to the UK for the TV meeting at Trafalgar Farm near Portsmouth. Sadly, on the rough Hampshire track the rather spindly suspension was not up to the task, and trying a little too hard Don crashed and broke two bones in his hand. More development was needed, but for the moment this was put on the backburner, because in the workshop countless hours were being spent planning and building the MkIII Metisse. In great secrecy during the winter of '61/'62, the new bike – which featured the first all-Rickman frame – gradually took shape in readiness for its debut at the Hants Grand National on Good Friday, 1962.

Resplendent in its lightweight glass fibre bodywork and nickel-plated frame, it looked a winner before it had turned a wheel – and to prove it went as well as it looked, the results of the first leg read "1st DJ Rickman, 2nd Jeff Smith, 3rd Dave Bickers." Hopes of a dream debut were denied when the Triumph-engined machine developed magneto trouble with Don leading the second leg, but the die had been cast; although Derek and Don didn't realise at the time, it was a watershed moment for them. Things would never be the same again.

Wins on the scrambles course on a Sunday had the spin-off of a sale in the shop on a Monday, and with the retail side of the business thriving the association with Bultaco began to gather momentum. Don found time for a trip to Barcelona to ride a 196cc Bulto in the 250cc Spanish GP, while at home a second MkIII with a Matchless engine was completed for Derek to debut in the Cotswold, in which he finished third. A Bultaco-engined 'Petite Metisse' with leading link forks had also been constructed, and as a wide-eyed ten year old I was lucky enough to witness both its debut at a Shepton Mallet event on the Mendips, and its appearance a couple of weeks later in the British round of the 250cc World Championship at Glastonbury. The latter was held over the long and demanding course at Higher Farm Wick, and on the little Bulto – which Don described at the time as being 'fast but fragile' – he had an inspired ride. In front of an enthusiastic 24,000 home crowd the younger Rickman finished a fine third behind Dave Bickers and Torsten Hallman in the first leg, but gearbox trouble in the second dropped him to seventh place, and fifth overall. Big brother Derek also shone at Glastonbury, winning both invitation races on the Matchless. As the season progressed, there was hardly a major meeting where the talented duo didn't figure first and second past the chequered flag.

Like the bikes that carried the name of Metisse before it, the MkIII had been made for the Rickmans' own use. However, as the wins mounted, their rivals became increasingly disenchanted with their

Derek on a Matchless Metisse at East Meon.

Derek on a 440 BSA Metisse at Bulbarrow.

uncompetitive Goldies and TriBSAs, and requests started rolling in for replicas of the beautifully crafted duplex frames. The demand suggested it could have commercial potential, so the decision was made to build half a dozen or so for friends. At that stage it was still their intention to remain motorcycle dealers, and not become manufacturers, but any hopes they had of remaining a small time operation disappeared after the MkIII Matchless appeared at the 1962 motorcycle show. A crowd of close to 180,000 flocked into Earl's Court, and at the end of the show the Rickmans returned to Hampshire with over 30 orders, including six from Denmark and others from France and Belgium. Things were starting to take off in New Milton, but as they quickly discovered, if they were to succeed it would be without the support or backing of the British industry's 'big three.' Hopes that BSA, Triumph, or AMC would supply them with engines or take over the manufacture of their frames were, as Derek told me, met with the same answer of "No thanks, not interested."

"Orders had reached 44, and with the workshop working flat out the only paper we had big enough to detail all of the production stages was a sheet of wallpaper. We felt that over a three-year period we'd proven that with the right engine the Metisse had shown it was capable of taking on and beating the best in the world. Some of our customers wanted complete bikes, but this was a major problem as Triumph, BSA and AMC all refused our requests to supply us with new engines. We then offered them the entire project free of charge, with the only proviso that they continued to let us have frames for our own bikes. We thought that as both Triumph and AMC had race-proven engines but decidedly ropey frames one of them would jump at the chance of taking on one with a winning pedigree, but neither showed the slightest interest."

Unlike their race track rivals from Small Heath, Meriden, and Plumpstead, who were 'professionals,' Derek and Don had to make a living from their business activities, and as a result they were never able to mount a serious challenge to the World Championship. Due to time and expense they were only able to compete in selective Grands Prix, but the results show that they were unquestionably two of the best riders in the world. There was decent money to be made from racing in France, but as Don told me, their desire to win in the continental GPs sometimes caused controversy.

"We loved racing in France because of the wonderful atmosphere generated by the huge enthusiastic crowds, and the organisers always put up some decent start or prize money. I recall that one year I won the 'Million Franc' meeting, and after being presented with my prize money – about £750 – I had to ride around the course waving it to the crowd. In the GPs we wanted to do well for ourselves, but it was also a golden opportunity to bring the Metisse to the world stage, so obviously we were keen to win. I remember after one early GP at Imola in which Derek and I finished second and third in the first race, we were approached by Harold Taylor who suggested that as we weren't championship regulars 'we can't have you winning this, and you've got to back off in the second leg.' Of course we didn't take a blind bit of notice of his 'words of advice,' and as ever gave it 100 per cent in race two!"

Behind the scenes there were also discussions going on with Bultaco, and just before the 1964 Earl's Court show the announcement was made that signalled the Rickmans were about to become manufacturers in their own right. The weekly publication *Motor Cycling* was first with the news that not only were the brothers about to produce Bultaco Metisse scramblers, but also market the brand-new 244cc Sherpa trials bike, which its creator Sammy Miller would continue to develop. The impact that Miller and the Spanish two-strokes would have on the world's trials scene is now of course legendary, but it is largely thanks to the business acumen of the Rickman brothers that it had its first public airing at that '64 show. Orders for 110 Petite Metisse, 70 Sherpas and 20 frame kits to the value of £100,000 were received, and with the business booming, a new company – Rickman Bros (Engineering) Ltd – was formed to look after all Metisse production and the Bultaco concession at a bigger factory site at Gore Road, New Milton.

Derek and Don were never short of energy, and in addition to racing virtually every weekend they also travelled to many parts of the globe promoting their race-winning machines. By late 1964 over 700 frames had been produced – half of which were exported – and six of the top ten finishers in that year's Motocross Des Nations team race were Metisse mounted. Spreading the net across the Atlantic the first big Matchless MkIII – weighing in at 280lb and finished in ivory fibreglass – appeared at a desert race in southern California, quickly showing that it was ideally suited to the requirements of the long-distance American races. This opened up another lucrative market for the Rickmans, but in the international races in Europe there was an ever growing threat from the big bore two-strokes. Throughout the '65 season – which saw Don beaten into second place by Belgian whiz-kid Joel Robert on his 360cc CZ in the Motocross Des Nations – debate had raged over the increasing presence of glorified 250s in the 500cc class, but as Derek revealed, nothing positive had been done to initiate a change.

"We weren't anti two-strokes, but felt the mixing of them and the four-strokes in the premier class wasn't good for the sport, so at Namur we organised a petition which was signed by nearly all the riders calling upon the FIM to resolve the problem. At their autumn congress they accepted our proposals and decided to create the new 750 Coupe d'Europe series for machines 501/750cc."

Member countries were invited to organise events for the 1966 season. Keen to see the new six-round championship succeed, the Rickmans built three 600cc Matchless and a 650cc Triumph specifically for the new series. Things kicked off in fine style with Derek notching two wins on the big Matchless in West Germany in May, but he had to wait until August before the second round in Switzerland. Lucky for him, because following a spill at Newbury he was forced to sit out the next three months with a broken shoulder, missing all of the important nationals, and also the home round of the 500cc World Championship.

Derek might have been missing from the Farleigh Castle line-up, but Don was out to prove he was not merely a 'bit player' on the world stage, and few of the sun-drenched 24,000 crowd will ever forget his performance that day. With the throttle of the Triumph Metisse nailed against the stop, he rode around the whole field on the first corner, and despite a late challenge from reigning world champion Jeff Smith he led the first leg from start to finish. With a break of barely an hour they were back in action again, and after Jerry Scott's bike expired on the first lap Don once again found himself in the lead. This lasted until half distance when he was overtaken by the BSA man, but try as he might, Smith was unable to break away, and as the flag dropped just four and a half seconds separated the two riders. After the cumulative times were checked and double-checked, the timekeepers announced that by virtue of his six second win in the first leg, overall victor of the 14th British Grand Prix was Don Rickman.

August saw the brothers back on the 750cc Championship trail to Switzerland, and despite riding with a swollen hand after he was stung by a wasp, Derek showed he was fully recovered from his broken shoulder and ran out overall winner, with Don a close second. After three more rounds on consecutive weekends, Derek led the championship trail by a clear 13 points from his nearest challenger, Erik Malmgren. Despite the fiasco of not receiving entry forms for the final round in Austria, he couldn't be beaten, and at the FIM's autumn congress D E Rickman was proclaimed 1966 750cc champion.

During the latter half of the 1960s the brothers' priorities began to change, and with the business ever expanding – this included a MkIV scrambler for the BSA Victor and unit construction Triumph twin, a 'street Metisse' kit, and a highly successful road-race tie up with Tom Kirby – there was less time for racing. Although the 750cc Championship continued for another year, it was without the Rickmans. Don continued to race the MkIV Victor in important races in the UK, but at the end of thc '68 season Derek decided it was time to hang up his leathers, and when Don followed suit two years later it brought the curtain down on two wonderful decades of scrambling for the brothers from New Milton.

It was the end of Derek and Don's racing careers, but it heralded the beginning of a new era that saw the Rickmans becoming the largest scrambler manufacturer in the UK. Tales of this and the beautifully crafted Montesa- and Zundapp-engined two-strokes exported to the USA are covered elsewhere. For now, it's thanks to Derek and Don for some wonderful memories of those golden days in which the Metisse reigned supreme.

Many thanks to Dave Gittens for allowing me to use extracts from his excellent book, The Rickman Story.

500cc British Motocross Grand Prix, Farleigh Castle, 30 July 1967. Don Rickman on a 441 BSA Metisse.

A very muddy Blackmore Vale trial in the mid-'60s. (Courtesy Gordon Francis)

During the 1960s Mary Driver competed at the highest standard in off-road sport, regularly up among the awards on her Greeves machinery, before becoming the ACU's competition manager.

CHAPTER 9

MARY DRIVER - AT THE TOP LEVEL

"Five minute wonder," and some gross indignation at the £2 price tag – this was Eric Buxton's response when his daughter, Mary, informed him that she needed a motorcycle helmet to ride pillion on her new boyfriend Dennis' BSA Gold Flash.

Little then in 1953 could Eric have guessed that motorcycling would be anything but a 'five minute wonder,' and that by the following decade Mary Driver would be known as one of the country's leading off-road female motorcyclists – good enough to earn the ride of a works Greeves in one-day trials, become a medal winner in the international six days trial, and a scrambler with the staying power and tenacity to finish in the top ten at the Twickenham clubs annual 100 mile grueller. In addition, her organising talents had also been recognised, and in 1966 she was appointed as competitions manager with the sport's organising body, the ACU, at its headquarters at Belgrave Square: a job she would carry out with aplomb and much respect for the next nine years.

Mary was born in north London and still lives just a few miles away in Hertfordshire with her husband, Dennis – the man who introduced her to motorcycling with his BSA A10 in 1953 – and as I soon discovered, she has plenty of clear and fond memories from those halcyon days of motorcycle sport.

"After I met Dennis, Dad insisted that I wore a helmet for riding pillion on the BSA. However, he wasn't so pleased when I told him it was going to cost him £2, as he was convinced that motorcycling and me was going to be a 'five minute wonder.'

"Dennis was – and still is – a keen motorcyclist, and during the '60s worked as a machine manager at Cornwall Press, the then printers of *The Motor Cycler* paper. I loved riding on the back of the BSA, but decided I'd like to have a bike of my own, so in 1954 went along to the RAC/ACU training scheme at Haringey and passed my test on a 197cc James. The same year I also got a secretarial job working with the ACU in Belgrave Square. By then Dennis had decided he fancied doing a bit of competition work, so he'd joined the Wood Green club and started riding in some trials, firstly on a James two-stroke and then later on a 500cc Ariel."

At that time the club organised several major events, including the Paley Cup, the Beggar's Roost, and Clayton trophy trials, and it wasn't long before the enthusiastic Mary was roped into helping out with some highly enjoyable tasks in which she covered many miles on her little road bike.

"I started following the trials, and after a while really got the

Mary on her BSA takes a crafty dab on Downscombe in the Wood Green Beggar's Roost trial. (Courtesy Gordon Francis)

bug. To begin with I helped out with the paperwork, and used to ride to events all over the country, including one in Derbyshire where I assisted Dennis in his job of clerk of the course for the Clayton trophy.

"After about three years' road riding experience I really fancied having a go myself, so with plenty of encouragement from fellow club members I entered my first event – a local club trial – on Dennis' James. I can't remember much about it now, but I can recall that although I managed to finish I didn't get on too well; I fell off several times and had lots of fives. We couldn't afford a car and trailer or a van, so for the first couple of seasons I rode the bike to the trial, competed, and then rode home again, covering many miles in the process. The first few trials were hard work but I loved it, and by the end of the season I'd won my first novice cup."

Riding to and from the events and fettling her bikes also gave Mary a keen appreciation for the mechanics of motorcycling, and with tips picked up from Dennis she became adept at wielding the spanners: skills that in future years would hold her in good stead when she started competing in the international six days trials. It also gave her a zest for speed, and the following year (1958) she competed in the MCC high-speed trials at Silverstone on a 500cc AJS, and again in 1959 aboard a 197cc DKW two-stroke. Little from the two events is now remembered, although Mary laughed as she recalled the look of shock on a marshal's face after a sidecar competitor had crashed. The rider was not seriously injured, but got up holding his severed leg: an artificial one ripped off in the spill.

1958 was a year for celebration. Not only was Mary showing steady improvement in her trials – winning her first first-class award – it was also the year that she and Dennis got married. By 1959 she'd progressed to a 250cc BSA C15T, and had begun competing in the important nationals, although by now the couple travelled in the relative luxury of a Bedford van.

"When I started riding in the nationals we decided to get a van and managed to buy an old Bedford from a fellow club member who was emigrating to Australia. I recall that they wanted £10 for it, but money was so tight for us at the time we had to send the money onto them later on. On the way to ride in my first Scottish in 1960 the Bedford overheated badly, and we had to stop and get some water out of a river and fill the radiator before we could carry on."

It was the first of her seven rides in the Highland six days classic, and as one of the few lady competitors, the smiling young woman from north London quickly became a firm favourite with the appreciative crowds. Riding for six hard days was no easy task, but Mary soon proved that she had both the skill and stamina to compete with the best.

In fact, she had improved so much that by the following year she had won an award in the national Hoad trial – qualifying her for Expert status – and earned sponsorship from Bill Slocombe.

"Dennis and I had bought all of our bikes from Bill, so he started sponsoring me in 1961 on a 250cc BSA – a bike prepared by Alec Wright, who was a wonderful engineer."

1961 also saw Mary Driver appear in her first international six day event on another Slocombe-sponsored 250 Beezer. It would be the first of five consecutive ISDTs for Mary, and for the 36th running of motorcycling's 'Olympics' she joined fellow lady riders Jill Savage and Maico-mounted Olga Kevelos on the Llandrindod Wells start line. There was a slight hiccup after she tried to start the BSA with the ignition switch in the wrong position on day one, but the Wood Green rider had a trouble-free week, and at the end of six hard days and 1200 miles of riding she came away with a well-deserved silver medal.

In one-day trials, Mary continued to compete with a great deal of success on the Slocombe-sponsored BSAs, although her luck was out in the 1962 West German ISDT, and she was forced to retire after she ran out of time following a spate of punctures.

In an effort to build up her strength and stamina, the same season saw Mary compete in her first scramble, and she was extremely pleased with her debut ride. "Dennis was then riding in scrambles – in fact he was doing quite well and had managed to get a 2nd in a local event on his Greeves – so I thought that it would be good to have a go myself to build up my upper body strength in preparation for the ISDT.

"I quickly discovered that scrambling was even more of a 'man's sport' than trials, but with my gear on no one realised I was a girl and in my first event I did quite well and didn't finish last."

There was no doubt that it certainly helped her prepare for the 1963 international in Czechoslovakia: one of the most arduous events in years, with a route so severe in places that Sammy Miller likened it to sections in a one-day trial. Mounted on a 250cc Greeves, the plucky north Londoner came away from Spindleruv Mlyn with a much-prized bronze medal. She now reflects on this performance as one of her best in all of her six internationals.

"After a long drive through Germany, we arrived at the border wire, and it took absolutely hours before we were allowed to cross into Czechoslovakia. We eventually got in and soon discovered it was like another world compared to what we were used to: little choice of goods in the shops, and secret police everywhere. We arrived at out hotel but there were no curtains at the windows, and we had to drape a spare blanket across the gap. The Czech people themselves were extremely friendly, but for the trial itself I was lucky to make the starting line.

"We discovered that my Greeves had a problem with the crankshaft, but fortunately for me a Dutch competitor – Simon Schramm – with a similar machine had crashed while practising and broken his leg, so before scrutineering we swapped motors, and despite the tough going it ran faultlessly for the whole six days. Looking back now, I think it was my best ever ride in an ISDT."

On a newly acquired 250cc Greeves, Mary also qualified for the 1963 southern Experts – carrying herself well in the trial – and shortly afterwards she was signed by Comerfords to ride works-supported machines: bikes that she would ride in both one and six days trials and scrambles with a great deal of success until her retirement in 1970.

"Although the bikes were sponsored by Comerfords they were looked after by the factory competition department, and I got to know Bert Greeves, 'Cobby,' and Bill Brooker extremely well. Both Greeves and Comerfords were great to work for, and if I'd had a particularly good ride they would send me 'well done' cards in recognition."

Her first season on the Thundersley two-strokes (1964) was certainly a highly productive one: successes included a silver award in the Scottish six days, and a trip to the near continent where she finished 20th out of 98 competitors in the International Trial De Forteresse, at Namur in Belgium. To prepare for the September international six days in East Germany, Mary also put in some memorable performances on the scrambles track – although one event left her very saddle sore.

"I loved riding in scrambles, and thought that the Twickenham club's 100 mile event at Pirbright would be ideal training for that year's ISDT in East Germany. Like the international, good machine

At a check point in the 1961 ISDT in Wales, on her way to a silver medal.

"RIDING FOR SIX HARD DAYS WAS NO EASY TASK, BUT MARY SOON PROVED THAT SHE HAD BOTH THE SKILL AND STAMINA TO COMPETE WITH THE BEST"

Mary lines up her Greeves on a tricky exit in the Bristol MC&LCC John Douglas trial, October 1962. (Courtesy Gordon Francis)

preparation was of paramount importance, but the mental attitude was equally important and it was no good treating it like a five-lap sprint. You just needed to be able to pace yourself, arrange support for fuel and refreshment stops, and most importantly, keep going. I did manage to keep going, and at the end of the race out of 77 starters I'd finished 9th – although my backside was so sore I couldn't sit down properly for a week!"

Steve McQueen was in the American team that year for the ISDT, and the whole episode of a Hollywood star behind the Iron Curtain created a lot of media interest. Mary recalls life behind the Iron Curtain as being very different to that at home, and remembers one thought-provoking incident where Olga Kevelos offered a child a banana, only to find that the child didn't know how to peel it. Olga was quickly pounced on by one of the local policemen, who told her that offering fruit to children was forbidden.

In what was classed a relatively easy trial Mary was forced to retire after a spate of punctures, but back at home she was a regular award winner on her Greeves in both open-to-centre and nationals, and was often pictured feet-up in the weekly Blue 'un and Green 'un. In 1965 she travelled to France to compete in the international St Cucufa trial, took part in the national scramble at Hawkstone Park, and just to show her versatility, rode a factory six days bike in a very wet Isle of Man ISDT.

In her day job, Mary continued to work as a secretary at ACU headquarters, but in 1966 she took on the new challenging role of competitions manager.

"The current secretary, Harry Cornwall, was retiring, so I decided to apply for the position and was absolutely delighted to be offered the job. Harry was a lovely man and was so much looking forward to a long and happy retirement, but sadly he died just a few months after he finished with the ACU."

In those days every road race, trial and scramble held in the UK fell under the jurisdiction of the ACU, and it was Mary's job to administer the decisions of the sporting committees and to make sure that all of the organising clubs were kept happy. In itself quite a daunting task, but on top of that, it was also her responsibility to help organise the TT, the long-distance national road rally, and sort out all of the logistics for the international six days trial teams. Understandably there was less time for her to pursue her own riding career, and due to being assistant secretary of the meeting at the TT, 1966 was the last year she rode in one of her favourite trials: the Scottish six days. As previously mentioned, Mary finished in all seven she entered and is justifiably proud of her achievements, but is the first to acknowledge all the help and encouragement she received along the way.

"It was fantastic to ride in the Scottish, but I owe much of my success to the skill, workmanship and support from the likes of Alec Wright [Slocombes], Bill Brooker [Greeves], and Bert Thorn [Comerfords] in preparing my bikes – they were very important people to me."

It might have been her last ride in Scotland, but she continued to compete in both one-day trials on her Anglian and the occasional scramble on her Greeves MDS: her husband's similar machine completing the Driver stable for 1966.

There was no ISDT ride for Mary in either '66 or '67, but the following year she was back in action on her Greeves in an event at San Pellegrino in the Italian Alps. Due to heavy rain making parts of the course impassable, it was super tough event, and Mary was one of the 13 British riders who went out on day one, being was forced to retire when her Greeves ignition system packed up. Although as she told me, actually getting to the start was not without its problems.

"I travelled by car and trailer with Jock Wilson from Comerfords, but when we arrived at the border the guards didn't want the bike entering Italy on a trailer, and insisted that we take it off, start it, and ride it across."

Battling over narrow rock-strewn mountain tracks against an extremely tight time schedule soon had many riders literally on their knees, although it was an electrical gremlin that brought an early end to what proved to be Mary's last international six days. She continued to campaign her Greeves in one-day trials until 1970, but with an ever increasing work load at Belgrave Square she decided to retire, bringing the curtain down on a memorable career. Although her own riding career finished in 1970, Mary continued to look after the interests of the international six days teams. She recalled an amusing incident from another trip to Italy in 1974.

"That year's ISDT was based at Camerino, high in the Abruzzi Mountains in southern Italy, and I went out some time before the trial to organise the team's accommodation. I looked around all over the place, but suitable hotels were pretty thin on the ground, and eventually we all ended up using a dormitory in an old monastery."

During our talk Mary told me many tales from her days as ACU's competition manager, enough to fill an article by themselves, but that will have to wait for another day. They were golden days for the young woman with the infectious grin, and ones she remembers as "the best time of our lives." It was certainly a good day when Eric Buxton agreed to buy his daughter a £2 motorcycle helmet.

To celebrate their golden wedding in 2008, husband Dennis is currently busy in his workshop restoring an A10 BSA. Motorcycling was certainly no five minute wonder for Mary.

Many thanks to Mary and Dennis for all of their help in compiling this profile, and for all they have done for motorcycling over the years.

A feet-up clean for Mary on the Greeves in the 1965 Scottish six days trial. (Courtesy Morton archive)

Mary tree-dodging on the 250cc Greeves in a local trial in Essex.

ISDT, Llandrindod Wells, 1954. One bump that hurt.

Arthur and Lyn Pulman were among Britain's top sidecar crews, winning the 1959 and 1960 British Championship before a dramatic change of motorcycle heralded a new direction for the sport.

CHAPTER 10

ARTHUR AND LYN PULMAN - PRIZE PAIR

Arthur Pulman was undoubtedly one of the best sidecar trials riders of his generation, and with his then-girlfriend, Lyn Britton, in the chair, he piloted his factory-supported 500cc Matchless to the British Championship title in 1959. This was repeated in 1960, and with the newlyweds now almost invincible it was naturally assumed that the same bike would be used to defend their crown in '61.

However, Arthur had his own radical ideas, and in a friend's garage in north London a new outfit gradually took shape. With Lyn perched on a wooden box, a lightweight sidecar chassis was built around her, and compared to what was considered 'normal' at the time the finished result was undeniably different. Up until then, virtually all trials outfits were powered by either a snappy single or a rasping four-stroke twin, so Arthur's choice of a lightweight 250cc two-stroke Dot was, to say the least, an unusual one. However, the Dot hadn't been his first choice: at that year's motorcycle show he'd approached AMC competition manager Hugh Viney to see if he could have one of the new 250cc model G2 lightweights to develop as a trials iron, but the idea drew a blank. Arthur and Lyn were at their peak and almost unbeatable on the 500cc Matchless single, so Viney couldn't see the need for a personal challenge – one that would jeopardise their chances of winning on an untried machine – and turned the idea down flat. The AMC boss clearly meant no offence, but Arthur was not going to give up on the idea of using a small capacity machine, and later a chance encounter with Burnard Scott-Wade saw him leave the show as an official works Dot rider.

At that time Pulman was working for accessory maker Doherty, and as he made his way back to its stall his eye caught the new trials model on the Dot stand. "Could you ride one like that?" asked a voice behind him, to which he replied "I'm sure it would be a real challenge." The voice belonged to Dot owner Burnard Scott-Wade, and within a few minutes Arthur was convinced of the bike's potential, and found himself signed as an official works rider on the Mancunian two-strokes.

He soon set to making a lightweight sidecar chassis, but when the outfit first appeared there were plenty of doubters who questioned his judgement – "You won't win anything on that" was a typical remark – but as the results soon proved it was an inspired choice, and one that during the next two seasons would bring the Pulmans plenty of wins and first-class awards. The trendsetting outfit was also a magnet for period photographers, and during '61 and '62 many images of the pair and the little two-stroke appeared in the weekly motorcycle papers,

On John Catchpole's unusual side-valve Norton special.

copies of which now adorn the walls of Lyn's home in Dorset. Sadly, Arthur passed away in August 1997, but it was great to meet up with Lyn who recalled some of those memorable muddy days on three wheels, and how she and Arthur first met.

"Back in the early '50s I needed transport to get to work, and despite my father's prophecy of 'you'll kill yourself on one of those things' I bought myself a 125cc Ambassador. Arthur – who had been born and brought up in Dorset – had moved to London with his work as an engineer, and we ended up working at the same company. He was already a keen motorcyclist, so when the Ambassador broke down he was on hand to repair it for me. We became good pals, and after a while I decided to try my hand at trials. We rode together in the Sunbeam 200 long distance event, but the Ambassador was painfully slow, and Arthur had to keep stopping and waiting for me to catch up. I joined the MCC and rode in the Lands End trial, and Arthur also used the little two-stroke in their speed event at Silverstone. By then we'd joined the local club, and on Sundays we used to go up to Bagshot Heath and compete in their popular one-day trials. It was there we met up with 'sidecar top dogs' Frank Wilkins and his wife, and Bill Slocombe and Arthur Humphries. One day Frank asked if anyone was interested in buying a Matchless and Watsonian trials outfit, so pretty much on the spur of the moment we decided to sell my Ambassador and give it a try."

Although a trials outfit was something new in the days before he'd moved to London, Arthur had already tried his hand at grass-track and had learnt to ride a fearsome 1000cc Royal Enfield known as 'Old Bill.' This belonged to his old friend Lew Coffin, who told me about those early postwar days in Dorset.

"Like a lot of the local lads, Arthur used to come up to my dad's farm where we used to tear around on our old bikes. I remember him riding around our test track in the moonlight testing out his Rudge grass-track bike, and after a while he got pretty good on a solo. He started coming to grass-tracks with me on my Royal Enfield vee-twin, the bikes transported alongside us on a flat-bed sidecar. At one meeting I crashed and broke my arm, so I told him 'you'd better learn to ride this.' So the first time he'd piloted an outfit was on this very potent 1000cc Enfield. He took to the sidecar like a duck to water, and also tried his hand on a speedway bike at Knowle in Bristol. He was a very talented rider, so it came as little surprise when in the '50s he started winning on a trials outfit."

It was 1954 when Arthur and Lyn won their fist novice award, and spurred on by their success they soon spread their wings to the nationals, and also that year's international six days trial in Wales. They returned from Llandrindod Wells with a much deserved gold medal, but as Lyn told me, competing in these events was hard and often cold work.

"In those days we couldn't afford a car or van to transport the bike, so we used to ride to all of the events. Typically, to maintain a decent speed on the road, Arthur would fit a different size rear sprocket, which he would change before the start of the trial. After the event the bike would be covered in mud and we were often cold and wet, but the wheel would come out again, the sprocket changed, and we would ride back home. Doing a national often involved riding hundreds of miles in a day. and something like the Scottish six days was an epic trip. The first couple of times we competed in the Highlands Arthur rode the Matchless all the way there and back, and I got a ride with some friends in a van. Arthur loved the Scottish but I must admit I didn't find it very enjoyable; there was a terrific amount of road work, and the trip out from Edinburgh to Fort William and the timed return seemed to take forever. The sidecars would be started off at random between the solos, so you didn't see most of your fellow competitors during the day, and it felt very much like you were riding around on your own. It seemed that every year we rode it was either raining or snowing, and at the end of the day we were like a couple of drowned rats."

Arthur and Lyn having fun on their 500cc Matchless (unknown venue).

Although the couple's trips to Scotland were largely memorable for aching bottoms and soaking wet riding gear, Lyn has some very pleasant recollections from their outings in Wales. They had some memorable rides in the country, and in the arduous Welsh three-days speed event they were crowned 'best sidecar' three years on the trot.

"It was hard work keeping to the time schedules, but the trusty Matchless never missed a beat, and we came away from our first event with the trophy for the best sidecar. In fact, we won the beautiful silver Welsh dragon trophy three years on the trot, and as a result hoped that we might keep it. I would have treasured it, but we were told that it wasn't due to the frugal nature of the organisers, but because the unique trophies were on perpetual loan to the mid-Wales centre from the Builth Wells club, and we had to be content with a replica instead. The Welsh was an extremely popular event with the chairs, and many of us would arrive at Llandrindod Wells a couple of days early and make a holiday of it. The trial was usually based at the Metropole Hotel in Llandrindod, and it was a great event; in fact, it was worth riding in just for the magnificent scenery alone."

On the national front Arthur and Lyn were regularly picking up wins and first-class awards on the Matchless, which caught the eye of

In the 1960 Scottish six days at Laggan Locks on the 500cc Matchless.

AMC competition chief Hugh Viney. He subsequently invited them to Plumstead.

"Hugh Viney asked us to go to Plumstead, and on arrival he asked us if they supplied us with parts, would we consider riding under their name? We readily agreed, and we also got some additional support from the likes of Avon tyres, Reynold chain and Shell which meant that if we did well in a national we would get a bonus payment of £5 or so which we saved towards getting married. Virtually all of our spare money went into keeping the bike going which meant it was 1961 before we could afford to tie the knot."

In their new status as 'works riders' the couple had also progressed to a Morris van which as Lyn recalled after the years of riding to and from the events was absolute bliss.

"After years of riding hundreds of miles to and fro events it was absolutely marvellous when we bought the Morris van, it meant that after a cold wet trial we could get out of our muddy gear, wash our hands and faces and drive home with the heater on! It also meant we could now ride in all of the nationals – even the ones in the far north – and in 1959 we won the British Championship (then known as the ACU star) on our works Matchless."

Against some formidable opposition Arthur and Lyn won the title again in 1960, were runners up to San Seston in the Scottish, and also took the outfit to the continent. Here they were extremely well received, and became friends with several German couples – friendships that lasted well beyond the day they retired from active competition. Tumbles competing in trials brought the inevitable cuts and bruises, but Lyn recalled that a crash on John Draper's farm the week before they scooped their first British Championship title was one of the most painful.

"We took the outfit over to John Draper's farm, and John asked if he could have a go at riding the sidecar. Sadly, going up a climb he tipped it over, and the grab bar hit me in the mouth. I lost four front teeth, and instead of going into the house John took me into the cow shed to wash my mouth out. Needless to say I was very 'gummy,' and didn't smile too much for several weeks. The worst injury I sustained in a trial was in the DK Mansell when my leg slipped off the support bar and got trapped between the sidecar and the road. I later had it x-rayed and they discovered I'd broken a bone, but it was plastered up and I continued to ride in events. The doctor was unaware of this, and couldn't understand how it was my plaster was always so dirt and muddy when he came to examine me."

In 1961 there were sufficient savings to get married, and when Arthur secured a job with Westland Helicopters the newlyweds moved back to the West Country. In later years at Westland's he progressed to training manager, being responsible for passing on his quality engineering skills to in-house apprentices. As Lyn told me, these skills were honed during construction of the works Dot back in the '60s.

"When we first got the Dot we didn't have a garage, so we took it to friend's house and I sat on a wooden box while Arthur measured everything up and constructed the sidecar chassis around me. One of our first competitive events was the 1961 Pierce Simon, and compared to the forks on the Matchless Arthur found the leading link forks to be very stiff. He fed this back to both Dot and the damper constructors, Armstrong, but they were hard to convince, so in desperation he fitted the front units upside down. This lost the main damp but made the action much softer, and later on Armstrong relented and made him some 'softer' units, which made a big difference to the way the bike handled and steered.

"Shortly after we got married in 1961 we rode in the Beggar's Roost trial, and spent our honeymoon in the pub which the organising club used as the start. To celebrate all of the riders clubbed together and organised a meal for us, but sadly some had too much to drink and a fight broke out. It ended up with everyone – including a couple of policemen – being chucked out, and as a result they decided to ban all motorcyclists. Years later Arthur and I drove past the same pub and the sign 'no motorcyclists' was still outside."

Although Arthur and Lyn didn't win another British Championship on the Dot, they did prove that sidecars didn't need the sheer horsepower of the big four-strokes, and during the next two seasons took many national awards. Many suggest it was Arthur who crusaded to put two-stroke sidecars on the map, but he always rejected that claim, and felt that the person who first made an impact was Brian Stonebridge, who he'd seen in action on his Greeves in the 1958 Scottish six days. Arthur certainly put a lot of effort into improving the Dot, and the MkII model – which had slightly longer front links and a new sidecar body – was a real leap forward. The way the attachment was spaced out made the whole outfit much more rigid, but it also meant that Arthur could use lighter gauge tubing, which saved a considerable amount of weight. He was also the first to build the chassis inside the sidecar body – this gave a smooth underbelly that helped it slide over obstacles – and he developed an L-shaped sidecar wheel support that gave maximum wheel articulation with minimal weight. On this outfit the Pulmans were narrowly beaten by Peter Wraith and his 500cc Ariel in the 1962 West of England trial in Devon, but it was one of Lyn's last outings in the chair. She was pregnant with their son Kevin, so she called it a day and Brian Dodge took her place in the chair.

"Brian was much bigger than me, so he found it difficult fitting into the custom-made chair on the Dot and after a few events Arthur decided to change it for something else. Brian Martin was keen to have him on a BSA and they supplied him with one of the new unit construction 343cc singles. Arthur and Brian had some good rides on this bike, including sixth in the 1963 British Experts trial at Llandrindod Wells, but by the mid-'60s Arthur's heart was not in the riding and he retired in 1965. Kevin had contracted cancer, from which he sadly died at the age of five, and it was time to call it a day and concentrate on family matters."

Later Arthur and Lyn adopted two lovely baby girls, beginning a new phase in their lives. It was the end of sidecar trials, but not the end of their motorcycling. There was usually a bike or two under restoration in the garage, and later when the girls flew the nest and Arthur retired, they undertook some fascinating two-wheeled tours to far-flung places like Morocco and Egypt.

Throughout their career there were few major trials that Arthur and Lyn didn't win, but during that golden decade the importance was not in the winning, but in the personal challenge and pure enjoyment of motorcycling. They were a great pair, and for those lucky enough to have seen them in action the sight and sound of that Dot squirming its way up a muddy section will live forever.

Big thanks to Lyn for all her time and hospitality.
Arthur Pulman 1927-1997

Runner-up to Sam Seston in the 1960 Scottish six days.

"VIRTUALLY ALL OF OUR SPARE MONEY WENT INTO KEEPING THE BIKE GOING WHICH MEANT IT WAS 1961 BEFORE WE COULD AFFORD TO TIE THE KNOT"

Typical Pulman neat and tidy style in the 1961 Clayton trophy trial.

1958 ISDT in Garmisch. Bill on his way to a well-earned bronze.

For close to 13 years, Bill Brooker was boss of the busy and successful comp shop at Greeves' Thundersley factory.

CHAPTER 11

BILL BROOKER - COMPETITIVE BUSINESS

Mention the town of Thundersley and any fan of '60s off-road sport will immediately associate it with Greeves, the small Essex factory that made such a huge impact in trials, scrambles and international six day trials events with its quirky looking two-strokes. Different they might have been, but there was no denying their success, and backed up by some clever advertising most bikes were sold even before they had rolled off the production lines. From clubmen to champions, there was never a shortage of people wanting to share in the glory, and the company's founders, Bert Greeves and his cousin Derry Preston-Cobb, were quick to acknowledge that 'a win on Sunday' usually meant 'a sale on Monday.'

Its period advertising gave the impression that Greeves was a much bigger company than it actually was, but there was no doubting the calibre of riders who raced and won on the little strokers. Some of the world's best became 'works-supported,' and at one time in the early '60s the comp shop had no fewer than 35 factory trials and scrambles bikes to look after.

Keeping all of the riders happy and the opposition at bay was not an easy task, and the man who donned the hat of comp shop manager was Bill Brooker. It was a challenging yet highly satisfying job, and Brooker held it for much of the 13 years he worked at the busy Essex factory.

The late '50s and early '60s were golden years for British motorcycle sport, and ones in which Bill worked with a plethora of world-class stars. These included the legendary Brian Stonebridge, European motocross champion Dave Bickers, Badger Goss, the Sharp brothers, and Don Smith. Some wonderful times, and 50 years on from the day Bill first set foot in the Thundersley works, I was lucky enough to talk to him – not only about those 13 years at Greeves, but also about his own riding career and love for motorcycling, which continues to this day.

Bill was already an established top-class one-day trials rider when he was invited to join Greeves in 1958, although as he told me, his own introduction to two wheels had come about some two decades earlier in the sands of the Middle East.

"It was the mid-1930s and I guess I must have been aged about ten or eleven. I was in Egypt where my dad was stationed in the RAF, and close by was my elder brother who was then in the army. He sometimes used to ride over to see us on his military bike, and would give me a ride around the camp on the back. It was great fun and then

1960 one-day trial in Holland. Don Smith won and Bill was best 250.

"BRIAN WASN'T BEST PLEASED THAT I'D USED ONE OF 'HIS' BIKES, IT WAS MY FIRST AND LAST SCRAMBLE"

1963 Dutch three-day international. Bill on his way to a gold medal.

one day he asked me if I fancied having a go at riding it myself: as you can guess it didn't take too long to say 'yes please.'

"I actually started riding 'officially' in 1941 after we'd returned to the UK, and I'd begun working for Alec Bennett's at Shirley near Southampton. On the outbreak of the Second World War the military had commandeered all unsold civilian machines from dealers showrooms, but fortunately Bennett's had been given the contract to look after the bikes on the army camp at nearby Romsey. After repair one of my jobs was to ride them back to the camp, which was great, so bitten by the motorcycle bug I decided to enrol into the Home Guard as a despatch rider. Later when the Yanks came – prior to the invasion of Europe – I got a job driving at their camp, and when I was old enough I joined the British army. They posted me on the motorcycle course at the specialist driver's wing at Blackdown, and when my training was finished they decided to keep me on as instructor. It was a great job, and over the next few years I trained lots of soldiers including Canadians and Dutchmen. The training grounds were over the rough terrain on Bagshot Heath; that really got me into off-road motorcycling, so when the war was over I decided to stay on in the army and started competing in trials. I later graduated to be an instructor training instructors, and one of my star pupils was Don Smith, a great rider who I would work closely with a decade later when we both were involved with Greeves."

During the early '50s the name of Bill Brooker featured in many one-day trials results, and he showed great versatility by being equally happy on a slogging side valve army bike or a specialised trials two-stroke. Along with Dougie Theobold and Gordon Norton he rode for the army in various team events, both at home and abroad, although it was his selection for the army team in the 1958 ISDT in Garmisch that secured his first ride on a factory-supplied Greeves.

"I was selected for the army on the Greeves, while my two team-mates were mounted on Dots; sadly both the Dot's packed up, and on the fifth day my bike developed gearbox problems. I spoke to Brian Stonebridge about it, and he said 'I'll listen to it when you come out of the Parc ferme.' It was making a click-click sort of noise which Brian diagnosed as a top gear pinion on the way out, and concerned that it could seize up suggested that I should pull out. Major Osmond – who was in charge of the army team – was concerned that, as the Dots had already retired, he might not get future funding for another ISDT effort, so asked me to carry on. The bike kept going but I lost marks on time, so on the last day I just needed to limp around for two laps on the special test to get my bronze medal."

Bill continued to ride his own Greeves with considerable success in one-day trials, and his talent had not gone unnoticed by Thundersley's boss man.

"I was riding in an event in Hampshire when I was approached by Bert Greeves, who said that 'when you come out of the army we would like to have you working at Greeves.' My army days were coming to an end, so I went to meet him and he offered me a job. He also asked if I would like to ride as part of the factory team with Brian Stonebridge and Jack Simpson in the next Scottish six days."

It was a good debut ride, and at the end of six hard days Bill came away from the Highland classic with the first of his five special first-class awards. Later that same year – 1959 – he also tried his hand at scrambling.

"I fancied a go at scrambling, so I asked Derry Preston-Cobb if I could use one of the spare factory machines. Brian Stonebridge was at that time experimenting with the NSU-engined bike on the continent, so Cobby suggested I borrow his spare Villiers-powered bike. He told me to make sure that I cleaned it before I brought it back, and I didn't think that Brian would find out. Of course he did, and wasn't best pleased that I'd used one of 'his' bikes, it was my first and last scramble.

"Brian got on really well with the NSU-engined bikes and wanted Bert Greeves to look at replacing the Villiers two-strokes with them, but Bert would have none of it. As I soon found out, once he'd made up his mind there was nothing anyone could do to change it."

When Bill started at the Greeves factory in late 1958, his boss told him to start at the bottom to get a feel for the way the company was run. Bill told me a little about this time and the way the bikes were made up.

"I started on sub-assembly with a number of jobs like constructing the front forks, putting bushes in the swinging arms, making up cables and fitting tyres. I suppose at the height of production there were probably 150 people working in the factory, and the bikes were made in batches of 20 or so, with each man on the assembly line making one machine at a time. All of the parts were put into bins and the assembly workers went along and picked out all they needed to make a complete bike. Typically they would make them in batches of 20 or so; trial bikes one week, scramblers the following week, and road irons the next. I had a go at most things, including the job of road tester – an interesting one, which involved giving the completed bikes a run and filling out a test report on each one before they were shipped off to the dealers."

With Brian Stonebridge, not only did Greeves have one of the world's best scramblers, but also a very clever development engineer. He was destined for great things, but when returning from the Hepolite factory in October 1959 Bert Greeves' car was involved in an accident, and Stonebridge was tragically killed.

"Bert Greeves was devastated by Brian's death, but things had to go on and Ernie Smith was taken on as comp shop manager. He was in the job for a few months, but he and Mr Greeves didn't always see eye to eye and when he left under a bit of a cloud Cobby asked me if I would take it on. I'd already managed to get my foot in the door when I worked with Brian preparing the bikes for the international six days, so I had a pretty good idea what it involved and decided to give it a try. I had a great team of people – John Pease, Dutchman Fritz Selling, and Chris Goodfellow – working with me preparing the bikes, and in addition to this it was my responsibility to sign new riders, and keep existing ones on board when they were approached by the likes of Husqvarna and CZ."

From the early days, Greeves was one of the few companies that had a dyno and experimented with various expansion exhausts – although as Bill recalled, not all of the good ideas were put into practice.

"The Greeves factory was a very happy place, but Bert Greeves could be very bloody-minded, and if he said no he meant no. He was very anti the NSU engine that Brian Stonebridge used for a while, and did his nut when he discovered that Dave Bickers had discarded the leading link forks for a pair of Ceriani telescopics, or that the same rider had changed his Amal Monobloc for a much better Bing carburettor in a continental round of the European 250cc Championships."

Being in charge of the comp shop meant that there was less time for Bill to pursue his own riding career, although he still managed to find the time to pick up a couple more ISDT medals. He won silver in a very wet event at Bad Ausee, Austria in 1960, and on home soil in Wales in 1961 he was a member of the British Vase B team, which finished a

Last day Bergamo three-day international. Bill won gold and Greeves scooped the team award.

1963. Left to right: David Clegg, Bill Brooker, and Alec Wright with the trophy from the Bergamo three-day international.

creditable third in the Vase competition. Both Bill and fellow Greeves rider Bryan Sharp won gold, although for Brooker it was a close-run thing, as on the fifth day he arrived at a control with literally seconds to spare. He initially thought he was over time, but kept his clean sheet, and with some spirited riding on the final special test he managed to accrue enough bonus points for a well deserved gold medal.

It was Bill's third and final ISDT, but he loved the enduro type events, and two years later turned up in Italy for the annual Valli Bergamasche three-day trial. Eighteen British riders made the trek southwards to compete in the Italian sunshine, and thanks to Alec Wright – who had organised them into national and manufacturing teams – the British line-up of Brooker, Monty Banks, Dave Clegg, and Don Smith beat the Polish team to take top honours. In addition, the Greeves line-up of Bill, Don, and Fritz Selling beat the German Hercules team to gain the manufacturer's award in this highly prestigious event.

In one-day trials Bill continued to ride both at home and on the continent, and won several first-class awards in top European events – events that he often travelled to with his works rider, Don Smith.

"I travelled to places far and wide, including the United States, which I went to with Arthur Browning in the late '60s on a sales tour. At home, Comerfords at Thames Ditton were probably our biggest customer, but the Americans loved our bikes and we had a good number of sales to both the east and west coast importers. They asked us for some weird and wonderful things, including desert bikes with 18in front wheels and huge petrol tanks. I remember we also made some special sheep farm bikes for Australia which featured a galvanised frame. This was so the farmer could ride the bike through the sheep dip without the paint being stripped.

"As a company we managed to sign some of the best motocross riders of the day including Bickers, Goss, Davis, and Wade, but by the mid- to late '60s things started to take a downturn. The profitable government Invacar contract – which had always kept the bike side afloat – was lost, and this coincided with Villiers' decision not to supply rival manufacturers with engine units. We were by then making our own engines for the scrambles bikes – although both the cranks and gearbox internals were made by Albion – so this was a devastating double blow. In addition, a lot of money had been spent developing the road racers, and we just couldn't make enough bikes to keep going. An engine unit had been sourced from Puch for the trials bike but it took a couple of years to develop it, and by the early '70s Bert Greeves had lost interest, Cobby was close to retirement, and soon the company was taken over by an engineering firm."

The writing was on the wall for Greeves, but the Thundersley bikes had always been well received in the States, and it was through an east cost importer, Ron Jekyll, that Bill landed his next job.

"The Americans loved the little 125cc enduro style bikes, but of course Greeves didn't have one, so Ron Jekyll asked me if I knew anyone in England who did. At that time I was still working for Greeves, but I knew Peter Edmondson at Dalseman was making some interesting stuff with small capacity Puch and Sachs engines, so I invited Jekyll over and took him to meet Edmondson. He liked what he saw and paid out £75,000 on an advance order, but a month or so later he phoned me and asked if I would go and check things out as he'd heard or seen nothing."

The result of Bill's visit was that there had been little or no work carried out on Jekyll's order, and following a court case in London the American became the new owner of Dalesman Motorcycles. Edmondson was kept on to run the export side of the business, and Bill was asked to leave Greeves and take over the running of the works.

"I'd worked at Greeves for 13 happy and successful years, and when I was leaving I went to see Cobby who asked me 'Where's your works bike?' Several former works riders had previously bought their old bikes when they finished, and I asked him if there was any chance of me buying it. His reply was 'Sorry I've already sold it.'"

Despite their modest engine capacity, the Dalseman trials bikes were surprisingly competitive, and in the Scottish six days the team of Gaunt, Wilkinson and Jefferies left many spectators open-mouthed with their performances on the little two-strokes. The Puch and Sachs engines had already proven their durability in enduro and motocross events. Housed in the Yorkshire company's frame, they were the choice of the British military team for the USA's 1973 ISDT 60th anniversary trial – a team managed by Bill Brooker.

"It was a tough event, and at the end of the six days only one of our bikes was still running, and it took Wilkinson to a silver medal. I suppose we were making about 25 bikes a week, but there was no way we could compete with the Japanese on prices, and after about three years it was obvious that we couldn't go on making them at a loss and decided to call it a day. The funny thing was that just before Dalesman packed up I was approached and asked if we would consider assembling Greeves bikes from parts supplied to our Yorkshire factory."

The demise of Dalesman brought the curtain down on Bill's trials career, and marked the end of his involvement with motorcycles for the next 21 years. For a while he was chauffer to a company in London, before moving to Florida. He then returned to Thundersley, where he bought and ran a garage for 14 years before retiring. However, it was not the end of Bill's trials career. At an age when most people are thinking about putting their feet up, he joined the Southend motorcycle club, and bought himself a trials tiger cub – the sort of bike he remembered with great fondness from his competition days with Greeves in the Scottish Highlands.

"I loved the sound of a cub at full chat up the pipeline, so decided to get myself one to ride in pre-'65 events. I've also had a modern Gas-Gas, but it was a bit too fierce for me so I sold it and got a 200cc Honda, which I now use in twin shock events."

His days at Greeves were obviously memorable ones, and in his role in the comp shop Bill made a major contribution to the company's success. Fifty years on from the day he first walked through the Thundersley factory gates, he still gets a lot of enjoyment from his motorcycling, and at the age of 83, must rank as one of the oldest active trials riders anywhere in the world.

It was a pleasure talking to Bill and recalling some of the memorable days of my youth, when the name of Greeves led the way in off-road sport. Many thanks.

1964 Dutch three-day international. Bill won gold.

"WITH SOME SPIRITED
RIDING ON THE FINAL
SPECIAL TEST HE
MANAGED TO ACCRUE
ENOUGH BONUS POINTS
FOR A WELL DESERVED

1959, West of England trial, on a 197cc Francis Barnett.

Beginning his career in the 1950s, Chris Cullen enjoyed much success during the 1960s, with his riding career stretching well into the '70s.

CHAPTER 12

CHRIS CULLEN - CULLEN TIME

It was the winter of 1956, and aboard a borrowed James – complete with 'Bobby Dodger' bicycle lights – a young Chris Cullen rode to compete in his first event: a southern centre novice trial. Like many aspiring trials aces his debut ride was a truly memorable one; not – like most of us – for tumbles and numerous fives, but for poise, style, and plenty of cleans. So many cleans, in fact, that when the results for the Southampton Vikings club event arrived some days later he was cock-a-hoop: on his first attempt, he had scooped the premier award. For the talented teenager it was the start of a long and highly successful trials career, which in the next twenty years would see the Hampshire man win countless other premier and first-class awards on a variety of machines; Francis Barnetts, Greeves, Scorpions, Cheetahs, Ossas, and Montesas, all ridden in the same feet-up, untroubled style.

The late '50s and '60s had a plethora of stars, all capable of winning an open-to-centre or national event; plenty of strong opposition. But during that time, there were few southern or south eastern centre events where the name of Chris Cullen didn't figure high in the results. To find out more about his one- and six-day trials exploits – and also his involvement as a works rider with Greeves, Scorpion and Cheetah – I met Chris at the Haynes motor museum in Somerset, where we relived some of those magical days. I began by asking him how he first became interested in motorcycles, and about that first memorable southern centre event.

"My dad was chief constable in the police force at Portsmouth and he never had any interest in motorcycles, but from an early age I fancied one, and got friendly with a neighbour, Jack Pinkney. Jack had a 98cc James Comet which he taught me to ride, and later on he progressed to a 197cc Francis Barnett, and then a James trials bike. I had great fun riding the James through the woods, and at the weekends started to go and watch a few of the local trials with Jack. I fancied having a go myself, so with the local Southampton Viking clubs novice's trial coming up Jack encouraged me to enter, and as I didn't have a bike of my own, I could borrow his James. I can't remember much about the trial itself now, but I recall that I had to fit some 'Bobby dodger' bicycle lamps to the front and rear, and rode it to and from the event. I had a pretty good ride with a number of cleans, but could hardly believe it when the results arrived and I saw that I'd won the premier in my first event. By that time I was apprentice printer at nearby Caustons, so soon managed to scrape enough money together to buy a Francis Barnett trialer from Jack White."

1962, Ashford Cup, on a 197cc Greeves.

The pukka competition Barnett had originally been purchased by White as one of a pair for him and his fiancée Gwen Wickham, and came with many of the ex-works Ariel man's home brewed modifications. Some of these – like the alterations to the steering head angle – were carried out in a rather crude way; a blowtorch flame played liberally onto the front downtube, and when the cherry red glow was judged 'right' the bike was forcibly wheeled into a wall. It might all have been rather rough and ready, but it worked, and soon the beret-wearing 'Cully' and the Barnett were regularly winning awards in the southern centre. One of the best was perhaps the outright premier at the prestigious Talmag in 1958.

For a while Chris rode the Barnett to events, but after he became friendly with Dave Freemantle the pair of them shared the luxury of Dave's Bedford van to transport their bikes.

After two hard seasons, the Jack White-modified Franny B was starting to lose its competitive edge, so in 1960 Chris bought himself a new 197cc Greeves Scottish. That same year he also received his national service call-up papers, although unlike many of his contemporaries – who had to put their motorcycling on hold – the army was quick to spot the young Cullen's talents. As well as spending the next two years in the service corps motorcycle team, he also rode in his first Scottish six days, competed as part of the services team in the 1961 ISDT in Wales, and was crowned army trials champion.

"Being in the army did little to hinder my motorcycling. In fact, it was great because I was instructing people on how to ride bikes during the week and competing in trials virtually every weekend."

Chris had been brought up on lightweight two-strokes, but soon showed his versatility by winning the Army Trials Championship on the standard issue side-valve M20 BSA and in doing so he beat some useful riders. These included BSA works man Dave Rowland and the talented Dave Coppock, the latter a clever man who would design and build the McClaren racing car, in which a decade later James Hunt would win his Formula One World Championship. The trio also scooped the services team award, and their victory was celebrated in style by their commanding officer who took them all out to dinner – something that was almost unheard of in the army.

His victories on the slogging single, however, weren't just limited to wins in army trials. He also kept a clean sheet to win the long-distance Hampshire 100 trial, an event organised by Ralph Venables, and described by Chris as being like a one-day ISDT.

He soon progressed to the ISDT proper, which that year – 1961 – was based around Llandrindod Wells in central Wales. He'd already given notice of his six-day potential with a scintillating performance in the Welsh three-day event of that year. Mounted on a works Royal Enfield Crusader, Chris came out top services rider, and in doing so beat some well known established aces like Peter Fletcher, Rowland, and Coppock.

When the teams for the ISDT were announced, Cully lined up with the two Daves – not on side valve M20s, but 200cc Tiger Cubs. The baby Triumph had already shown some ISDT potential, but as Chris told me, with persistent oiling and overheating problems they were hard-pushed to deal with six days of Welsh mountains and bogs.

"The cubs looked purposeful enough, but in the international they developed all sorts of problems, and gradually fell apart under us; of the six entered, Dave managed to win gold and I got silver, but the rest fell by the wayside, including one which seized solid on the last day's special test."

The trial was reported on by *Motorcycling*, which lamented over the results, saying "it was not a good advertisement for British Motorcycles."

It would be ten more years before Chris rode again in the international six days, although he recalled that in the Isle of Man 1971 event, he only got as far as the second day before crashing out.

"I was then riding for Bob Golner, and he'd entered me on an American style 360cc Yamaha desert racer. Instead of the 21-incher I was used to it had a fat 18 inch front tyre, which made it difficult to ride. I guess I was trying a bit too hard and crashed it in a big way, and ended up in Nobles hospital."

Tiger Cubs were again the army's choice for the 1962 Scottish six days team, which comprised 'Tiger' Timms, Steve Johnson, and Gordon Norton, with Chris selected as reserve. It seemed that his Scottish debut would have to be put on hold, but undeterred, Chris went with the team to Scotland, where lady luck was smiling on him.

"I wasn't expecting to ride, but went along in my Morris Minor pick-up with my private Greeves in the back. It was my intention to ride around on the Greeves as a spectator, but on the day of signing on Peter Stirland didn't turn up. I don't know how they managed it, but Major Eric Davey – a super bloke who looked after the team – and Bill Brooker from Greeves wangled me a ride, and with a new set of tyres supplied by Bill I got to compete in my first Scottish six days.

Having finished runner-up to Gordon Jackson the previous year, the '62 trial was eventually won by Ariel-mounted Sammy Miller, but it was a memorable week for the young Cullen – after six wonderful days, he lost a total of 83 marks and went away from the Highlands with the best newcomer award.

With national service over it was back to civvy street for Chris. He returned to his work as a printer and more one-day trials successes. In the southern and nearby south centre, the Greeves-mounted Cullen was the man to beat. Not only was he winning open-to-centre events, but he was also getting himself noticed in the local nationals, and finished well up in the Hoad, John Douglas, and Knut events. After a superb ride, he was also runner-up to Don Smith in the Perce Simon trial.

Throughout his 20-year riding career Chris rode a variety of machines, but one of the most interesting was perhaps the works Scorpion: a bike that, in 200cc guise, he rode to a second-class award in the 1963 Scottish six days.

"The bikes were made by a chap called Paul Wright. He was a keen trials rider, but he'd made a name for himself as a highly successful chassis designer in the cut and thrust world of racing cars. I've got a feeling he'd done some work with Lotus, so his bike was based around a monocoque type space frame as opposed to the conventional round tube and lugged affair used by the other British motorcycle manufacturers of the day. He was based near to the Silverstone race circuit in some workshops which had formerly been used as two storey pigsties. I went there and was amused to see the bikes ridden down the plank from the top floor to the ground. It was an interesting looking machine, and after trying it out I agreed to ride one for him."

Both Chris and fellow works rider Jon Tye rode the Scorpion with some success, although there were some problems with the frame design along the way – little wonder that the bike soon earned the nickname 'biscuit tin special.'

On the 250cc Scorpion in the Scottish six days.

"I MANAGED TO GET TO THE FINISH, BUT LATER DISCOVERED THAT THE WHEEL BASE HAD BEEN GETTING PROGRESSIVELY SHORTER AND THE BIKE HAD ALMOST COLLAPSED UNDER ME"

On the Lawton and Wilson 250cc Greeves in the 1966 southern Experts.

Chris on the Bob Gollner Ossa, in the 1972 Bishops Walton trial.

"We were asked to evaluate the bikes – which were still in prototype form – in events like the 1963 Scottish six days and British nationals. I remember taking mine to the Traders trial in Wales, but couldn't understand why the chain kept going slack. I managed to get to the finish, but later discovered that the wheel base had been getting progressively shorter and the bike had almost collapsed under me. Because of the lightweight frame the bike weighed in at just at a tad less than 200lb, and had an almost perfect centre of gravity. It wasn't quite so good over rocks, and later Paul had to extend the swinging arm by an inch to transfer more weight onto the front end, which had a tendency to bounce and be easily deflected."

With a new aluminium petrol tank and Marcelle top end conversion, Chris took the 200cc version to Scotland in 1963, coming away with a well deserved second-class award. It was an impressive little bike, and having learned some lessons he returned a year later on the new Parkinson conversion 250 to win a first-class award, although he recalled it was thanks to Arthur Lampkin that he made the start.

"Just before the Scottish the bike had been supplied to me in 'kit form' in a tea chest. We built it up, but when I got it out of the pick-up at the start the front fork damper units fell apart. Fortunately they were the same as fitted to Arthur Lampkin's Cotton, so he gave me a pair which got me to the start and through the trial."

Production Scorpion trials, scrambles and a clubman's road racer would be made later, but the company died with the demise of Villiers in 1966, and by then Chris had long since moved on.

"I've got a feeling that later on Paul turned his talents to making Daleks for the BBC, but by then I'd got myself a ride on a factory-supported Greeves. The Thundersley factory were supporting lots of people then, so my bike wasn't anything special, and I rode it for a season before I moved on to a Bob Golner Cheetah."

The Villiers-engined Cheetah featured a chrome frame and was one of the first trials bikes to feature a disc front brake. Constructed by Mick Whitlock and Bob Golner it was a very competitive machine and one on which Chris recorded quite a few wins including the hard fought southern centre Time Trials Championship. It would also see the start of a long friendship between Golner and Cullen which has lasted to the present day. After the Cheetah Chris was sponsored on a couple of Greeves supplied by Lawton and Wilson; machines on which he rode to first-class awards in the Scottish six days and one of which won him a bet with the legendary Ralph Venables.

"I liked the power delivery on the Greeves, but didn't take to the banana front forks, so I got Lawton and Wilson to change them for a pair of Cerianis which suited me much better. I was riding it in a West of England national and got to a section where Ralph was observing the action.

"'No cleans yet,' said Ralph 'and I bet you won't be the first.' 'Ok,' I said, 'and what are you going to give me when I go clean?' At that time Ralph was heavily involved with the Sunbeam club, so he replied 'I bet you the Sunbeam club subscription that you won't go clean.' 'OK,' I said, and with the Greeves lined up absolutely perfectly recorded the first feet-up climb of the day. Needless to say Ralph was gobsmacked, but true to his word he later paid for my next year's subscription to the club."

The days of British bike supremacy were coming to an end. Not only were three new major challengers emerging in Spain, but the demise of Villiers heralded the beginning of the end for the likes of Greeves, Cotton, and DOT. Chris had seen some good days on the Lawton and Wilson-sponsored Greeves, but if he was to remain competitive he needed a new bike, and this soon came in the form of a Golner-sponsored MAR Ossa. A change of job saw him move to Trowbridge and the Wessex centre, with new mud-plugging rivals in the form of the young Geoff Parken, Martin Strang, and the popular Frome clubman Mike Aven. By now – the early 1970s – Cully was perhaps just past his best, but he was still capable of winning an open-to-centre event, and many an aspiring rider learnt a lot from watching his smooth and uncomplicated style. He would continue riding bikes supplied by Bob Golner right up to his retirement in 1977, by which time he was riding a 348 Rathmell Montesa – a bike that over thirty years later he's still got in his workshop.

After calling it a day Chris rode in a few local classic trials, but that's not quite the end of the Cullen trials story. More than a decade after his last ride, the bug started to bite again. In the winter of 2007 he bought himself a very tidy looking 500cc Triumph trialer, so we might once again see the name of Chris Cullen in the results.

There is no doubt that Chris was not only one of the leading West Country riders of his generation, but also one of the most popular; many of his former rivals and old friends will be pleased to see him back in the saddle. There were many highlights during his 20-year career, but for Chris, winning both the individual and team award on the army issue M20s stands very high on the list. "As was," he adds with a smile, "the heartfelt thanks from the CO who took the winning team out to dinner to celebrate."

Many thanks to Chris for all of his time, enthusiasm and help in compiling this profile.

In the 1974 Jersey two-day event on his 250cc Montesa.

Somewhere in Wales on a 500cc BSA Gold Star, circa 1957.

For over 50 years Bill Gwynne has ridden and driven in two- and four-wheel motorsport, excelling in everything from lightweight Spanish two-strokes, to British heavyweights and rally cars.

CHAPTER 13

BILL GWYNNE - OFF-ROAD PRINCE

He was still a fresh faced 14-year-old schoolboy when he rode in his first event: a local time and observational trial in 1954, on his father's 197cc Dot. From the outset it was obvious that the lad had talent, although even he was a little surprised when he learnt that he'd beaten the entire field – all adults – to scoop the premier award.

It was a memorable start to his competitive motorcycling career, but greater things would soon follow. Still not 15, he was thrust into the tough world of scrambling, and before he'd reached his 20th birthday he was riding a Fred Rist-sponsored Greeves and had taken his 500cc BSA Gold to Welsh Championship titles for three years on the trot.

Between 1954 and 1972 Bill Gwynne raced a variety of machines, and was unquestionably one of the greatest Welsh scramblers of his time. He was born in Welshpool in mid Wales in the early years of World War II, although at the end of hostilities the Gwynne family moved to Cardiganshire, and it was here that the teenage Bill made his competition debut in 1954. The following two decades would bring him countless wins in both the UK and the near continent, but it was at the Higher Farm circuit at Wick near Glastonbury that I first saw him in action in July 1962. It was the setting for the British round of the newly announced 250cc World Motocross Championships, and on his factory Greeves Bill lined up against some of the world's best.

Later on in the 1970s he swapped two wheels for four, and became an accomplished rally driver, winning no fewer than five major championships. For the last 25 years he's run a very successful rally driving school at Brackley in the Midlands, and it was here I caught up with him to relive some memories from his illustrious motorcycling career. I began by asking him about his early days, and that first memorable win.

"I think it was about 1953 when my dad – who prewar had done a bit of road racing – turned up with a trials Dot, which I soon put to good use riding around the local woods. I loved sliding about on it, and the following year decided to enter my first event. This was a club time and observation trial at nearby Bromwydd Park and I had quite a good ride, but when the results arrived I was amazed to see that I'd won the premier award: a little trophy that I've still got to this day."

Spurred on by his success in the time trial, Bill soon rode in his first scramble – still aged just 14. This was again on the trials Dot, although to deal with the rigours of racing the little two-stroke was now

sporting some major improvements to the frame, and to get a ride he fibbed to the organisers about his age.

"Dad was friendly with John and Pip Harris, and they carried out some modifications which included fitting some beefier front forks and a rear swinging arm. I had no way of getting to the event, so the local blacksmith volunteered his services and took me in his Austin Seven Ruby car, on which he towed a homemade trailer carrying the Dot.

Of course I was still under age but told the organisers I was 16 and I guess they must have believed me.

I had a decent ride but undoubtedly the highlight of '55 was a scramble at Llanllwch where I managed to win three races. I was over the moon, but when I got back home my family wouldn't believe me until the results arrived the following week."

By now the trials Dot had been pensioned off and replaced by a purpose-built scrambler – also a Dot – and the young Gwynne was becoming a force to be reckoned with. Sadly, Bill's father died when Bill was only 15, but with a trailer attached to the family car his mother took over the driving duties, and the name of Bill Gwynne soon spread across Offa's Dyke into England. It was time to think about a better machine, so in 1956 a trip was made to John Avery's shop in Oxford to secure a brand-new BSA Gold Star. Bill recalled that, fitted with the scrambles air filter, it cost a whopping £234 17s, but it was the most potent piece of machinery around at that time, and he chose a fitting place to run it in: the support races at the British Grand Prix at Hawkstone Park.

"Seeing the Hawkstone track for the first time at 15 was a bit daunting, but in the support races I did OK. Compared to the Dot the Goldie went like the clappers, and I managed to finish third in the first race and fifth in the second."

On leaving school Bill had landed a job as an apprentice at the Royal Aircraft Establishment at Aberporth, but he quickly discovered that success on the scrambles track meant double the earnings compared to the RAE. Not an easy life though, and Bill recalled that a typical Easter programme was the Hants Grand National on the Friday, Pembrokeshire on the Saturday, Cumberland Grand National on Sunday, and Southend on the Monday. Huge mileages spent covering the length and breath of England, which – in pre-motorway days – quickly wore out his Bedford Workbus.

Welsh scrambling in the early '50s had been dominated by the likes of Tommy Wheeler, Cyril Rogers, and Cyril Hawkins – but Hawkins was beaten by Goldie-mounted Gwynne in 1957, and such was his domination that two further championships came in '58 and '59, making him the first and only person ever to win three titles in succession.

His achievement and huge popularity were also recognised outside motorcycling, and following his win in '59 he was voted Ministry of Defence sportsman of the year. This was a great award, as it allowed him ten weeks' unpaid leave. Vital time, as he had nothing else to prove in the Welsh Championship, and it meant he could expand his riding horizons to England, Ireland, and Europe.

The 500cc Gold Star had been joined by a 250cc Greeves supplied by Fred Rist, and it was these two bikes Bill raced at his continental debut near Caen in 1959. Some British riders found it difficult to break into the lucrative French meetings, but some tips from fellow Greeves rider Mike Jackson paid dividends for Bill.

"I got some good advice on what to do and where to go from Dave Curtis and Eric Cheney, but Mike Jackson told me to 'use your own headed note paper with your results typed on and it will impress the organisers.' I got my sister to type it out and the very first one I sent off was accepted. From my home in Wales to the ferry terminal at Dover was about 325 miles each way, but my £120 start money was enough to cover all of my travelling expenses, and having the two bikes meant that I could usually win a bit of prize money on top of that."

Wins in the national meetings on the Rist-sponsored two-stroke soon saw Bill mounted on a factory Greeves: a move that made him Thundersley's youngest works rider, and a partnership that, despite the offer of a works BSA, would last for four happy years.

"Although my Goldie wasn't a factory bike I got some help from BSA and got on well with both Bert Perigo, and later on, Brian Martin. They offered me some limited works support, but it was on their 250, which I felt wasn't as good as the Greeves two-stroke, so I turned them down. During my four years with Greeves I got on particularly well with Bill Brooker and Bob Mills in the comp shop, and also with Derry Preston-Cobb: Cobby was dead straight and a great man to deal with."

During those four years Bill was part of a formidable team of top class riders comprising himself, Dave Bickers, Bryan Goss, Triss Sharp, Joe Johnson, Mike Jackson and Alan Clough, and despite the stiff competition he notched up numerous wins on the Thundersley two-strokes.

In 1960 he finished runner-up in the 250cc British Championships on his Greeves, but travelling from his base in Wales was a long tiring business, so when the opportunity of a job working at Dave Curtis' motorcycle shop at Bicester presented itself in 1961, he didn't need a second bidding. Managed by former ISDT star Eric Chilton, it was an ideal base for the ambitious Welshman, and it also gave him the opportunity to try out some different machines, including a Matchless Metisse, an ex-Ron Langston Ariel, and an unusual Michou – the latter with an Ariel engine mounted in a BSA frame.

Throughout his racing career, Bill's neat and polished riding style meant that crashes were kept to a minimum, but he recalled a couple of nasty ones – spills that kept him out of action for several months.

"I think it was in 1961, and I'd been picked to ride in both the Motocross Des Nations and Trophee Des Nations teams, but I had a bad crash in France and broke my collar bone, which meant I wasn't fit enough to race in the international team races. Later on – I think it was 1966 – I also had a very bad crash at Thirsk, although at the time I didn't realise how serious my injuries were. After racing I set off driving home, but was in so much pain I had to hand over the wheel, and when I went to the hospital the following day I was told I was lucky not to be paralysed. They discovered I had a fractured skull and a broken neck, so I was put in a neck-to-waist plaster cast for four months. As you can imagine, after all that time I was a bit smelly."

Although Bill was primarily a scrambler, he also enjoyed the occasional trial. In fact, he was good enough to win a couple of open-to-centre events, although he readily admits his do-or-die antics often left both him and the bike looking rather secondhand.

"While I was riding for Greeves I asked Cobby if I could have a trials bike to keep fit during the winter. He agreed, and I decided to enter the St David's national. I was in a group riding around with Sammy Miller, and while Sammy was making it look all very easy I seemed to be having lots of fives and plenty of crashes. I was OK

Bill aviates the 250cc Greeves in the invitation race at the Motocross Des Nations.

"BILL BECAME A MAJOR COMPETITOR IN NATIONAL AND INTERNATIONAL RALLIES, SCOOPING FIVE MAJOR TITLES"

Bill leaps the 250cc Greeves at the 1962 World Championship meeting at Glastonbury.

on sections where I could give it a bit of 'welly,' but pretty poor at the nadgery stuff, and at the finish the bike was looking decidedly secondhand – so much so, when I handed it back to Cobby he said that he'd never seen such a battered machine after only one trial."

Thanks to exposure from the television scrambles series during the winter, the name of Gwynne was soon spread to a wider audience, and there were few 250cc races where he didn't feature in the first three. In 1963 he was a member of the south Midlands team that finished third in the annual inter-centre team scramble, and the following year he made the first of his four appearances representing the south, in the north versus south at Cross-in-Hand in Sussex.

Throughout his career he was equally happy on a quarter-litre two-stroke or a booming four-stroke single, and his list of 'bikes raced' is a very interesting one.

"During the late '50s and early '60s I rode all sorts of bikes, including a 250cc Dot, Roger Kiffin's Triumph-engined Dot, the works Greeves, a James, and a Starmaker-powered Royal Enfield. I was invited by the James comp shop manager to try their new bike, but as I soon discovered it was too long and bulbous; in fact, it would probably have been better as a trials bike than a scrambler. Along with Mick Bowers I raced the Starmaker Enfield at some TV scrambles during the winter of '64, but although it was pretty fast it suffered from a lot of clutch slip which was never fully sorted. Also during '64, Chris Carter arranged for me to do an evaluation on a 250cc twin Honda scrambler, but as I quickly discovered it needed a lot of work, and after reporting this back to Honda it was never seen again.

"Although I raced a lot on 250cc two-strokes, I loved the big singles, and after the Goldie became uncompetitive I scrambled a 500cc Matchless Metisse for a couple of seasons. This was a super bike to ride, but it was hard to keep on the pace with the new breed of big bore two-strokes, so I decided to pension it off for a new 360cc Bultaco Bandito."

After four very happy and successful years with Greeves, Bill was now on a Bultaco-engined Metisse in the lightweight 250 class – but his season with its bigger brother was not a long or happy one. "I had quite a few wins on the little Metisse, but the standard 360cc Bandito was awful and I just couldn't get on with it. I only had it for one season and then got rid of it."

Much to the chagrin of many fans and riders, big bore two-strokes were taking over in 500cc class racing. So – in England and Sweden, at least – there was joy when the FIM introduced its new championship for 1966. Generally known as the Lundin plan, it was an effort to combat the spread of the two-strokes, and was open only to four-stroke machines with an engine displacement of between 501-750cc.

Ever an enthusiast of the big bangers, Bill was quick to sign up. He raced in the British round at Brands Hatch in '66. With an over-bored, 504cc, ex-Dave Curtis Matchless engine in his Rickman Metisse, he was soon 'on the pace,' and at the end of a hard day's racing he finished in a creditable sixth place.

Spurred on by his success, he decided to contest all of the rounds in '67. With the bike firmly strapped in the back of his pick-up, he travelled many thousands of miles across Europe in pursuit of championship points.

On the booming, blood-stirring Metisse – which had now grown to a full 600cc – he recorded some impressive and consistent results over the next two seasons. His efforts were rewarded in '68 when he finished as runner-up to Sten Lundin in the final table. Don and Derek Rickman had been great supporters of the four-stroke 750cc Championship, but outside the UK and Sweden it had been met with only lukewarm support, and there was little surprise when it was dropped at the end of the '67 season. For Bill it was a return to two-strokes, and for the next four years he raced 250, 360 and 400cc Husqvarnas for their importer, Brian Leask. Although the inevitable 'anno domini' was catching up, he took to the Swedish strokers like a duck to water, and at all of the major southern events during the late '60s and early '70s he was still one of the top riders.

Throughout his 17-year scrambling career, Bill's smooth riding style meant that serious injuries had been kept to a minimum, but in late '72 he sustained a painful back injury and decided to call it a day. He retired from scrambling that year, but it was not the end of his racing career – he opted to put a roof over his head, exchange two wheels for four, and take up rallying. Skills learnt from two decades of racing Dots, Gold Stars, Greeves, and Metisses were soon put to good use, and over the next ten years Bill became a major competitor in national and international rallies, scooping five major titles.

In 1982 he opened his now highly successful rally school – at that time the first in the country – but the love of motorcycling was never far away, and in 1996 he was lured out of retirement.

"Derek Edmonson persuaded me to have a go at enduros, and told me that the Breckland was the 'one to do.' I couldn't believe how difficult it was, and if I could have found my way back to the start instead of sticking to the route it would have been my first and last enduro. I did a few more, and by then enjoyed them so much I decided to compete in a few scrambles, so I dug my old Husky out of the shed and joined the Southern Motocross Club. Surprisingly, I did quite well, so later on I progressed to a KTM, and ended up winning their Over-60s Championship. In fact, I won three times on the trot."

Over 50 years have now passed since that first memorable win on his father's Dot, but some things never change. Bill Gwynne – first past the flag, and judging by the grin on his face, obviously enjoying himself.

Many thanks to Bill for all of his time, help and enthusiasm in helping me to compile this profile.

On the 250cc Greeves Challenger at the Dorset Grand National, Bridport.

In full flight on the 360cc Bultaco Bandido at Newbury Fox and Hounds.

A grass-track outing on the GWS in August, 1963. Freddie Wilkins is keeping the chair wheel down. (Courtesy Morton archive)

As sidecar motocross enjoyed increasing popularity in the '60s, Mike Guilford was one of the leading exponents, racing and helping build some of the sport's most successful outfits.

CHAPTER 14

MIKE GUILFORD - GUILFORD'S GUILE

As the motocross sidecar crews lined up for the final round at Beenham Park in 1968, only a single point separated championship leader Mike Guilford from his nearest challenger, Nick Thompson. As befits a championship finale, it was an epic race, and with two laps to go the two main protagonists, plus John Turner, approached the infamous Beenham mud hole, with Guilford and passenger Malcolm Lamden holding the lead. In the gooey morass disaster struck for Guilford when he stalled his rasping Triumph Wasp, and as the Wiltshire man struggled to restart he was passed by three of his rivals. It looked like the British Championship had been handed to Thompson. However, Guilford and Lamden were not about to give up, and with a superhuman effort passenger Lamden lifted the whole bike high enough for his driver to kick-start it back into life. Within half a lap they were up to third, and ahead lay Thompson and Turner. As the three outfits approached the mud hole for the last time, Guilford – with the Wasp flat-out – decided it was do-or-die and took an unorthodox line. They showered the huge crowd with mud and Mike hit his head on an overhanging tree, but he stayed on, and in doing so not only managed to pass both of his rivals, but also keep them at bay for the rest of the lap. The championship silverware was his.

By the time of this victory Mike Guilford had been racing motocross sidecars for the best part of ten years. I first saw him performing at the same Beenham circuit in the summer of 1962. To find out more about Mike's racing career and his lifelong involvement with sidecars, I visited him at his Wiltshire home where we spent several hours reliving some of those halcyon days of scrambling.

Mike made his official scramble debut at the age of 18, although he was only 14 when he first took to the race track.

"All of my older brothers were into grass-track, so from an early age I would ride in their sidecars around our back field, although I was only nine when I rode my first solo.

"My brother's sidecar was a bit of a hybrid, featuring an unknown stationary engine – which came from a scrapyard – fitted into a BSA Sloper frame with a hand gear change operated by a lever behind my leg. I rode this around the nearby fir plantation until I was about 14, when I got my first race as passenger to Arthur Spencer. Arthur's passenger had broken his leg playing football, and although I was officially too young to race my mum gave me the OK and I guess the organisers must have turned a blind eye.

"I rode with Arthur on and off for a couple of seasons – including

Mike and Fred Wilkins on the 650cc GWS at Hawkins Bottom, 1963. (Courtesy Gordon Francis)

some speedway – and by then I'd started work as an apprentice in the nearby military workshop. I fancied a go at speedway myself, but I had little money, so decided to go scrambling instead. Fred Wilkins agreed to passenger for me, and we entered our first event in the sand at Pirbright in 1959. Our homemade outfit was based around a 1939 Red Hunter frame, and powered by an ex-speedway JAP engine prepared by the well known Nelson Harring. It was pretty quick and we actually led off the line, but after a couple of laps we hit a tree stump and broke the Burman gearbox. The engine was sounding a bit rough so I took it back to Nelson, who told me the cylinder was totally knackered – all because we'd been racing it with no air filter fitted."

Both Mike and Fred were apprentices with little or no money, but thanks to Fred's boss, Ralph New, they travelled to the events in style, giving the impression to the opposition that they were extremely well-off.

"Ralph New was extremely keen and he was also a very good organiser. He used to transport our outfit to the various meetings aboard his Austin A70, and saw to all of our paperwork and entry forms. He did this for the first two or three seasons until he got married, and I can't begin to thank him enough for all of his help and enthusiasm during that time."

During that time sidecar motocross was getting extremely popular, and most weekends the duo of Guilford and Wilkins were in action at events organised by the Reading, Winchester, and Portsmouth & Petersfield clubs. The combination of Rufus and Tiger Rose was the one to beat, and by the end of his third year Mike was good enough to be more than a nuisance to the pair. He recalled that he was forced to move his oil tank to the left hand side of his bike after one close encounter with Rose almost removed it from the offside and also the first time he beat him.

"It was at an event at Bridport and I beat him fair and square. I remember that Ralph New was absolutely over the moon and was dancing around as the chequered flag fell. I also did a couple of grass-tracks on my scrambler, and although riding a scrambles outfit was allowed, the grass-tracking fraternity didn't like it – especially when they got beaten by one"

Mike's day job in the military workshop was an ideal place to fabricate bits and pieces for his outfits, and it was a secure position. However, the young Guilford found it somewhat institutionalised, and he was soon looking to move on. Shortly after finishing his apprenticeship he saw his perfect job in the motorcycle trade, and went to work for Peter Stirland in nearby Marlborough.

"I was about 22 when I saw that works Enfield trials star Peter Stirland was opening a new shop in Marlborough; He was a good bloke to work for and I stayed with him for about twelve months before moving on to Tommy Edwards motorcycles in Luggershall. Tommy was extremely well contacted and it wasn't long before he got me sponsorship with Avon tyres and Castrol."

The sponsors were soon getting their money's worth when in 1962 Guilford won the British Experts Grand National at Rollswood Farm; victory in this trade-supported event brought him more contracts from Reynolds chains, and also from Girling suspension units. His bike had now been christened the GWS (Guilford/Wilkins Special), and although now powered by a Triumph twin engine and featuring leading link forks it was still very much a derivative of the original. In 1960, along with Roy Price, Mike had been one of the first scramblers to use leading link forks on his JAP. Although fairly crude, they were an undoubted improvement over the conventional telescopics.

For the many of fans who followed scrambling in the '60s, Mike Guilford was a name we instantly associate with Wasp. Mike told me how he first met the company's founder, Robin Rhind-Tutt, in 1962.

"I really felt I was on my way after winning the British Experts in '62, and that year along with friends Ralph and Fred formed the ACU-affiliated Kiwi Motorcycle Club. One of its first members was Robbie Rhind-Tutt, who at that time was working at the Boscombe Down military site and had just started racing on the grass.

"Robbie and I soon discovered that we had very similar ideas about making racing sidecar outfits, so we went ahead and constructed one. We built the whole frame from scratch, based on geometry from my previous bike, and incorporated a set of trailing link forks which I designed and made myself. It looked good but it took a while to get it right, because although it was fantastically light and steered well it was very skittish to ride. It really motored, which meant I could still win on it, but Freddie Wilkins didn't like it – this was largely because the sidecar chassis layout prevented the passenger from moving about freely. We rode it for a season, but by then Fred had started his own business and decided to retire, so Dave Bowman took his place in the chair."

The young Bowman was very brave, and ideally suited to Mike's full on riding style. With various improvements to the RT-GS bike – redesigned forks and increased ground clearance – the Guilford/Bowman duo were virtually unbeatable during 1965.

At the end of the year they won the TV meeting at Beaulieu – a victory that impressed rival Bob Golner. For some time, Bob had been badgering Mike to sell him the impressive outfit, and at the end of the meeting told him he desperately wanted it; he would pay him good money, but he wanted it dirty, just as it was. By then Mike was working for Sid Lawton, and the RT-GS sported some special gearbox internals supplied through Francis Beart. Sadly this was unknown to Golner, who after racing it – and during a subsequent rebuild – substituted the box for another from a 650SS road bike he was preparing for sale. Much to Bob's consternation, he ended up with a standard Norton gear cluster, while the new 650SS owner had a one-off special with international cogs.

£450 – quite a bit of money in '65 – changed hands for the RT-GS, and with it Mike and Robbie built the first outfit to wear the soon-to-be-famous name of Wasp. Over the decades Wasp would become very much associated with that of sidecars, although as I discovered, the first bike to wear the name was a solo.

"I was doing some engine work for George Sawyer – who at that time was selling quite a few Metisse frames – and he suggested that Robbie should make a similar solo frame to that the Rickmans were producing. This he did, and we were all looking at the finished result when someone said 'what we going to call it then?' George's brother in law Peter was with us, and piped up with 'Wasp.' He drew it freehand on the petrol tank, and then added Rhind-Tutt underneath to create the very first 'official' Wasp."

It would be the start of a long association between Guilford, Robbie Rhind-Tutt, and Wasp. Although they had plenty of new ideas, executing some of them left Mike scratching his head with frustration.

"We wanted to save weight with the new outfit, so we based the design on that of the solo which had a 2in shorter wheelbase than the

Mike on the 650cc GWS at a muddy TV scramble at Beaulieu, February 1962. (Courtesy Gordon Francis)

"WITH VARIOUS IMPROVEMENTS TO THE RT-GS BIKE THE GUILFORD/ BOWMAN DUO WERE VIRTUALLY UNBEATABLE DURING 1965"

On the 650cc Wasp at Newbury in June 1969 with Fred Little in the chair. (Courtesy Morton archive)

previous bike. There was no denying that with its nickel frame and yellow fibreglass the finished thing looked fantastic, but the practice session at East Meon proved it was a bit of a disaster. With its trailing link forks it was much too short, and it was obvious to everyone watching that all was not well. I shrugged it off as 'just an off day,' but it needed some serious work to make it competitive. We fitted a longer swinging arm and got it reasonable, but I struggled during most of the '66 season, which put us out of contention for the British Championship. The championship was won fairly comfortably that year by Len Crane, with us a distant third."

With lessons learnt, a brand-new Wasp outfit featuring a longer swinging arm and mid-frame was wheeled out for the following year; a bike that would be the basis for the first production machine. The fit and extremely strong Malcolm Lamden had taken over duties in the sidecar, but once again Crane took the championship. In fact, Guilford and Lamden would have to wait until the last round of the '68 season, and that thrilling last lap dice with Thompson and Turner, before they scooped their first British Championship title.

Guilford went on to win again in '69, but as he soon found out, Nick Thompson was going to be an extremely difficult man to beat.

"Thompson was becoming a bit of a nuisance – very fast, especially downhill, and at one of the early season meetings at Brill I just couldn't stay with him. I came to realise that the 68 degree steering head on our Wasp was too upright, whereas the 63 degrees on Thomson's BSA-based frame gave increased stability. Robbie decided to change our head angle by cutting and rewelding the top tubes, but this gave other problems. The first thing that happened was that the bottom race in the steering head burst out, and then the stanchions broke. In the first round at Chard, Malcolm had come out of the chair and broken his wrist, so I lined up at Hawkstone with Robbie's brother-in-law Fred Little as passenger. Fred was a forester – a big strong man – and totally raw at passengering, but although he was completely knackered we managed to finish third in the first championship race, and within two or three weeks he was very competitive."

During 1969 the British champion and his new passenger were invited to race in France, and were soon very popular with the Gaelic crowd. However, the French courses featured some seriously high jumps that showed the limitation of the trailing link forks.

"It was great racing in France as they paid some good start money, but most of the courses had some big jumps, which played havoc with the trailing link forks. The steering geometry didn't allow good suspension unit movement, which meant that halfway up their travel they would pass 90 degrees, so if you whacked them hard after landing from a jump they would get stuck. I was getting through suspension units galore, and although the trailing links worked well enough at speed we decided to make a leading link, which proved to be a vast improvement."

The French crowds loved Mike's all action style but the home crews were usually left floundering in his wake, so much so that he recalled how one of the organising clubs offered him an 'incentive' to make a bit of a race of it.

"We were in an event near Toulouse when after the first race the secretary of the meeting sidled up and offered me an extra 200 francs if, in the second leg, I could arrange to get bogged down at the start and then play catch up to entertain the crowd. This I did, and with the crowd yelling just managed to overtake the leader on the final straight and win by a bike's length. The whole atmosphere of the racing in France was commercial with good start money, but very relaxed and we were expected to entertain. I absolutely loved it."

Mike loved it to such an extent that in the 1970 season he didn't bother with many rounds of the British Championship – in which he finished 4th – and instead opted to go over the channel, where he won 25 races on the trot.

With all the experience he'd gleaned from racing on the continent, Mike fancied his chances when the European Sidecar Championship was announced for the '71 season. However, his newly constructed 750cc Triumph engine proved less than reliable.

"Instead of keeping with the reliable 650cc Triumph engine, I decided to make a bigger 750 motor with a Norton crank, but it wouldn't accelerate the same as the old bike and I just didn't like it as much. Then, with a week to go, my passenger had to pull with domestic problems so I went to the first round in France with Ronnie Emms in the chair. Ronnie was a young and very fit welder in the factory but he'd never passengered before. We had to tell a few fibs to get him a licence, but despite a fall in practice Ronnie did well, and I think we finished 10th and 11th in the two legs which were won by Nick Thompson.

"We didn't do many of the British Championship rounds, but persevered with the European rounds – although it took a long time to sort out what the problems were with the 750 engine. We eventually discovered that the crankcase breather was allowing air to get into the frame tubes, the oil was vaporising and the result was that we were wrecking engine after engine. I was fed up and considered retiring but Sid Hartle had a word with Robbie and managed to persuade him to supply me with a complete rolling chassis. This was fitted out with a Norton Commando motor which, thanks to engine builder Dave Ludswell, had much better breathing. This meant that it ran the whole season without being touched, and I managed to finish fifth in the European Championship."

When travelling to the European rounds, Mike often had his friend and rival Nick Thompson as a passenger in his 190 Mercedes diesel. The well-packed Mercedes carried five passengers, two bikes on the trailer, a sidecar on the roof, another jammed between the two bikes, and all of their riding kit, thousands of miles around Europe.

At the end of the '72 season and after 20 years of racing, Mike and passenger Mick Ripper called it a day. Mike then spent a couple of years working as team mechanic to John Player Norton, before being made redundant and lured back to Wasp, where he helped design and develop its new RT 15/RT 17 outfits.

Mike raced for another two years with passenger George Skeates, but by then he was past his best, and after suffering a broken leg and wrist he eventually retired from racing. Not that this was the end of Mike's involvement with Robbie Rhind-Tutt and Wasp. He continued to work with them on and off for many years, and in the early 1990s was very much involved with the design and construction of their superb road-going outfit, and is still friends with Robbie to this day.

It was also not the end of the name 'Guilford' featuring in sidecar motocross results. Son Martin started passengering in AMCA events at 14, and two years later scooped the AMCA Championship. He too went on to become a top class rider – on bikes made by his father.

Many thanks to Mike for all of his time and hospitality in reliving those wonderful days of sidecar motocross.

Mike and Fred Little on the Triumph Wasp at the international.

Mike (on the Wasp) leads Dave Fox at Gurston Farm, October 1967. (Courtesy Morton archive)

On the 125cc BSA Bantam in his first national, the Shropshire Cup in 1953.

In a career that spanned more than 20 years, Ken Sedgley rode a whole host of exclusively two-stroke machinery in a wide range of off-road events.

CHAPTER 15

KEN SEDGLEY - TWO-STROKE STALWART

In a career that started on a rigid framed three-speed 125cc BSA Bantam in 1953, Ken Sedgley went on to become one of the most successful trials and scrambles riders of his generation, and nearly six decades on he's still a regular sight around the Midlands competition scene. For the last 30 years Ken has worked in association with Silkolene oils as a 'lubricants consultant,' but for those who followed trials and scrambles during the '50s and '60s he is best remembered for his all action, never-say-die riding style on a variety of very potent two-strokes. His successes – including an ISDT gold medal – were all achieved on 'strokers,' although as I discovered, the works specification Greeves, Husqvarna and CZs he raced in the '60s were very different to the humble Bantam on which he served his competition apprenticeship.

The early '50s was a time when the young Ken had aspirations of becoming a county cricketer – his local club sent him to Edgbaston for coaching – and he also bought his first West Bromwich Albion season ticket, but a trip with his father to the 1953 TT whetted his appetite for two wheels, and within a month he had his first bike.

"My dad had a road bike and was a member of the West Bromwich motorcycle club. He was pally with Bill Evans, Bill Boddice, and Vic Artus, and started taking me to grass-tracks at Rushmere and other nearby circuits. He also took me on holiday to the Isle of Man, and after seeing the likes of Geoff Duke scorching around on his Norton, and all the thousands of enthusiasts with their bikes, I decided it was time to get my own. A month later I bought a road-going 125cc Bantam and went to spectate at some of the local trials. Jeff Smith and John Brittain made it look all too easy, so I decided to have a go myself. A specialist trials bike was out of the question, so I decided to treat the Bantam to some knobbly tyres and entered my first event. This was the Bridgenorth club's national Shropshire Cup trial on 30 August, 1953. If I recall, Don Evans was the winner on five marks with Jeff Smith runner-up on six, and although I lost a lot of marks I managed to struggle round and finish."

Although Ken finished out of the results on his debut trial, he was soon expanding his riding horizons. In the days before he had a pick-up or van to transport his bike, his 'multipurpose' Bantam covered a lot of miles.

"As an apprentice, running a car or van was out of the question, so the Bantam was used for everything – trials, scrambles, riding to work, and even taking the girlfriend out. I remember one of my earliest

Trying very hard on the works Greeves, 1962.

On the 250cc Dot in the national John Douglas trial, 10 December, 1964. (Courtesy Gordon Francis)

events was at Church Stretton for the Victory trial. Church Stretton was the best part of 50 miles from my home so I rode the bike to the start, took the lights off, competed in the trial, put the lights back on, and rode home again; around 150 miles in the day on a three-speed 125!"

His scrambles debut also came in the summer of 1953 at Feckenham near Redditch, where once again the Bantam was ridden to the start and then stripped of silencer, lights, and number plates before being raced. Shortly after he also competed at Hawkstone Park, but the fearsome course defeated the little BSA, and it was time to look for something more competitive.

"The Bantam was reasonably OK on fairly flat circuits, but on steep climbs it ran out of steam, and at Hawkstone I never managed to get up the main hill all day. The DMW factory was not too far away – between Dudley and Wolverhampton at a little place called Sedgley – so in 1954 my parents loaned me the money to get a new bike. This was a 197cc DMW – complete with plungers and lightweight teles – which we bought from sidecar trials expert George Buck in nearby Wednesbury. I started picking up a few awards, and after about a year or so I got a bit of help from Mike Riley – prewar, Mike had been a BSA works rider and now rode for DMW – and the factory boss Arthur Frost. Impressed by my performances, they asked me to take my bike back to the factory where they fitted it with a pair of heavier duty MP forks. If they'd given me a million pounds I couldn't have been happier."

The next two seasons saw plenty of trials and scrambles where the name of Ken Sedgley featured in the results, and by 1956 he'd progressed to an ex-works James: a bike he rode to a special first-class award in the first of 12 consecutive rides in the Scottish six days trial. His travelling companion to that year's Highland classic was Roy Peplow, who like Ken was starting to make a name for himself – he would eventually become one of the leading all-rounders of his day.

"Roy had started on his trials career on a 147cc Francis Barnett, and I remember he immediately looked very useful. When he was called up for his national service he joined the army motorcycle training unit at Aldershot, and it was there he was spotted by Ralph Venables. Ralph had lots of influence within the factory competition departments, and recommended Roy to Henry Vale, who immediately signed him to ride a works Triumph. In later years Roy and I travelled many thousands of miles together, but I think we went to that first Scottish together because at that time he was one of the few of us who had any transport, and he volunteered to take me and the James in his pick-up. On the scrambles front I also raced an AMC-engined James for a while, but it was an awful bike and I soon exchanged it for a DOT which I got from sidecar scrambler Len Crane. I had a bit of success on the Dot, but as an engineering apprentice at Birmetals money was tight, and I had to get by on what was a fairly motley collection of bikes. Although I continued to work at Birmetals I got a part-time Saturday job working at Tom Swallow's motorbike shop in Oldbury, and it was thanks to Tom I got my first big break in 1958."

Swallow was a Greeves agent, and, impressed by the youngsters dashing riding style, he quickly recommended Ken to Derry Preston-Cobb. Preston-Cobb also liked what he saw, and soon Sedgley was added to Thundersley's line-up of works riders. Now on a 'proper bike' – initially a 197cc, updated to a square barrel 250cc in '59 – the wins soon started coming. Although if he had a couple of poor weekends, 'Cobby' wanted to know why.

"I got on really well with Derry Preston-Cobb, but they expected me to do well in every race I rode in. At that time it was their policy to support a rider in each area. They supplied the bikes and spares, leaving their man to get on and win races. They had high expectations, and if the results showed that I'd been beaten a couple of times by someone like Ernie Greer, Cobby would ring me up and ask what was wrong. He would usually finish the conversation by saying 'if you can't do something about it can you get me Ernie's phone number and we'll get him to ride it.' They didn't pay me any money, but on a typical weekend I would race in the Welsh centre on Saturday and either the Midland or western centres on a Sunday, and would often come home with £40 in winnings in my pocket. In my day job at Birmetals in 1959/60 I was then earning £4 10s, a week and even the fully fledged fitters only took home around £11, so they thought that I was a millionaire when I started to turn up at work with my new pick-up. At that time it was almost unheard of for one of the workers to have a car, so as there was no allocated space I used to park it in the bosses car park."

Greeves didn't just supply Ken with a works scrambler; he also had the latest trials iron, but competition in the Midland centre was extremely tough and every weekend it was like riding in a national.

"Every Sunday I was riding against the likes of Sammy Miller, John and Pat Brittain, Brian Povey, Jeff Smith, and Scott Ellis, which meant it was extremely difficult to get into the top ten. Often I would have what I considered to be a good ride – losing perhaps 18 or 20 – only to discover someone like Scott Ellis had only lost two or three."

The popularity of winter time TV scrambles brought motorcycling to a whole new audience, and in the early '60s there was barely a 250cc race where the tenacious Sedgley and his works Greeves weren't found battling for the lead. One particularly memorable meeting was a two-day Cheshire centre event at Marple Bridge, where in some atrocious weather conditions Ken brought the Greeves home in the first three of all his six races, winning two of them. The same year – 1961 – he won the Isle of Man Grand National, and also took the step of opening a motorcycle shop at Northfield. Initially the show room was full of BSAs and Ariels, but as a trained engineer Ken had a keen eye for quality, and it wasn't long before the first Hondas appeared.

"I went along to the Earl's Court show in '63 and was immediately impressed by the little C100, which when compared to things like the Raleigh Wisp looked to be the perfect commuter bike. I think the on-the-road price of the C100 was then £79, so I decided to order nine. With the giant Austin car plant only a mile from my shop I had no shortage of eager customers, and I sold out in a couple of weeks. Later on I got some CD 175s which, with their electric starters, flashing indicators, and oil tight engines, were so much better than a 175 Bantam, but sadly the British industry had its head firmly in the sand. I recall a visit from one of their reps who was very dismissive of the new bikes from Japan, and told me in no uncertain terms that if I wasn't prepared to stock the whole range of BSAs, Ariels, and Triumphs then he wouldn't let me have any bikes at all."

On the competition front Ken continued to notch up scrambles wins both at home and on his occasional visits to the continent, but at the end of 1963 his successful association with Greeves came to an end, and he was looking for another ride.

"1963 was a good year. Pat and I had got married, the shop was going well, and I'd managed to keep winning on the Greeves, but I guess that half of me fancied a change of machine, and this came about

Ken leads from Mike Hicken and Stuart Wiggins at an XHG meeting at Giant's Head.

Ken on his way to winning the 1966 Welsh three-day trial on the 250cc Greeves.

after I test rode the new Challenger, which Greeves were planning to release for the '64 season. I took one to Hawkstone Park for testing, but compared to the previous bike it seemed big and cumbersome, didn't handle as well, and I just didn't like it.

I was friendly with Pat Lamper, and for a long time he'd been pestering me to ride for Dot, so I went up to Manchester for a meeting with Bernard and Michael Wade. I must admit that at that meeting they didn't seem to be very interested, but the following day I got a phone call from Bernard and he said 'are you serious about this?' I said I was and they let me have a couple of scramblers and a trials bike. Sadly the whole Dot thing was a total disaster. Although they handled reasonably well on bumpy circuits, they were left standing by the new Challengers and, it was obvious that more engine performance was called for.

"Understandably Greeves wouldn't sell me any bits, so I bought a new Challenger, took the head, barrel and exhaust off, and put them on the Dot. It made the world of difference and I was now quick enough, but I couldn't keep it all together – the clutch went, the gearbox stripped cogs, the chain snapped, and I couldn't finish a race. The Challenger had an alpha bottom end and a Swedish Steffa magneto, so Vale Onslow let me have a similar Miller mag for the Dot. The first time I raced with it was in a Wolverhampton scramble at Kinver, and at the end of the first lap the Dot was going extremely well and I was in the lead. Sadly, on the second lap it stopped dead when the Villiers main shaft broke and the Miller mag went into orbit. We couldn't find it, but a week or so later someone brought it into the shop. I was determined to make it both competitive and reliable, so I got Norman Cutler at Alpha to make me a full circle crank with a Steffa mag. The Alpha crank was much stronger, but of course it still had the Villiers gearbox, which under acceleration would strip its cogs for a pastime, and I ended up carrying a supply of spare gears in my toolkit which I would change between a heat and a final."

In one-day trials the Dot was proving to be much more reliable than its scrambles sibling, and Ken was still able to pick up first-class awards in open-to-centre events, but the Spanish invasion was now under way. Almost overnight the British two–strokes were uncompetitive, and aboard a 250cc Bultaco supplied by then-importers Don and Derek Rickman he recorded his best ride in the Scottish six days, and also won several premier and first-class awards in important open-to-centre and national events. 1965 also saw Sedgley make his debut in the international six days trial in the very wet Isle of Man, but despite his best efforts his bike only lasted to day four, when it eventually cried 'enough!'

"Alan Kimber was a great ISDT enthusiast, and had ridden a 175cc Lambretta to a bronze medal in Wales in 1961. In the mid-'60s he was working for Suzuki, who had set up their UK base in the James factory site at Greet, and he asked me if I fancied riding one of their bikes in the '65 six days. They prepared five T10-based 125cc two-strokes for the trial, but these were little more than road bikes with a bash plate, a slightly turned up silencer, and trials tyres. I had nothing to do with preparing the bike; I just turned up and rode it. On the road it was painfully slow, and I had to ride it virtually flat out the whole time. On day one I remember the route turned right up a narrow twisting back road heading up onto the mountain, and I could see a bike ahead of me. I tried everything to catch it, and eventually managed to squeeze past just before the checkpoint up near the bungalow. It was only when the rider pulled into the check that he realised he was on a 50!"

Like the other 125cc Suzukis ridden by fellow Birmingham club members Olga Kevelos and John Stone, Ken retired on day four. However, it had whetted his appetite, and the following year he was mounted on a much more purposeful machine.

"Despite the weather and riding an uncompetitive machine I enjoyed the six days on the island, so decided to enter the following year's Welsh three-day trial. I got a ride on a Greeves which I borrowed from the factory, and amazingly I won, which meant that I automatically qualified for the 1966 ISDT in Sweden. Much of the course was on rocky tracks through dense woodland, but the Challenger-engined bike ran absolutely faultlessly for all six days and I won a gold medal."

Following John Harris' win on the Super Six in the '67 Welsh, Ken was enticed back into the Suzuki ranks for that year's ISDT in Poland, but as he recalled, a two-stroke twin – which regularly became a single – was not the most perfect off-road machine.

"After John Harris had won the Welsh, he, Peter Gaunt and myself were given them for the ISDT. The trip to Poland was memorable as Peter wasn't overly confident of finding the way, and made the whole trip with his Austin Westminster virtually glued to our trailer. Only once did he become detached from us, but in trying to catch up he failed to notice we had stopped around a corner at some traffic lights and couldn't stop in time. The car slithered into our trailer, and although there was no great damage he flattened the long tail pipes on the two Suzukis. Later, near Salzburg, he backed his trailer into a hedge so no-one could pinch the bikes, but in the hedge was a brick wall so his pipes were flattened as well."

In the event proper Ken's very peaky twin kept running onto one cylinder, which caused his eventual retirement. It would be another four years before we saw him in ISDT action again, when he rode an Ossa in the Isle of Man. This again resulted in retirement, but in the meantime there was a busy shop to run, and still more trials and scrambles to compete in.

Disenchanted with the Dot, Ken had gone in search of something fast and reliable – and it wasn't long before he found what he was looking for.

"By the mid-'60s the first Huskys and CZs were creeping into the UK, and after seeing Joel Robert performing on his CZ I ordered one from Mick Berrill in Northampton. There was a three-month wait, so in the meantime I bought a Husqvarna from Jack Hewitt, which compared to the Dot really flew.

"On time as promised, the CZs duly arrived, and I took to them like a duck to water. You could slide and drift them with ease, and they were just terrific bikes. They were so good, the following year – early '66 – I asked Dave Bickers if there was any chance of him getting me a twin port 360, and a couple of weeks later he phoned to say it had arrived. At that time I think it was the first non-works 360 in the country, and in my first event – a Malvern clubs event at Castlemorton – I romped away from the field and won by a mile. If I remember correctly it cost me £330 with spares, and within a couple of months I'd got my money back. I rode it summer and winter for the next two years and it was an absolutely brilliant bike. Without doubt the 250 and 360cc CZs were the best bikes in my whole scrambling career."

With his smooth and polished riding style a Sedgley crash was an unusual occurrence, but after tangling with the ropes at an Abergavenny meeting at Cross Ash in August 1969 – in which he suffered a broken nose and a badly burnt neck – Ken decided it was time to call it a day.

Another shot from the TV scramble at Glastonbury in 1965.

1969 Scottish six days on the 125cc Sprite.

“WITHOUT DOUBT
THE 250 AND 360CC
CZs WERE THE BEST
BIKES IN MY WHOLE
SCRAMBLING CAREER”

On the works Dot at a Midland centre event in 1964.

It brought the curtain down on his scrambling career, but he continued to compete successfully in trials, rode in the 1971 ISDT, and also became a top-notch competitor in Formula Ford and later Formula Three racing cars. In this second phase of his competition career, Ken won races at home circuits like Mallory Park, and also competed at Monaco, Paul Ricard, and Estoril, supporting the Formula One Grand Prix. Although he had hung up his scrambling leathers at the end of '69 he was tempted out of retirement in 1972, and found himself spending five happy weeks racing in the heat of southern Africa.

"I was riding in the Vic Brittain trial – I remember it was a bitterly cold day – when I bumped into Malcolm Davis who told me he was off to race Bultacos in Zambia the following week. In an off-the-cuff remark he asked me if I fancied joining him, so after the trial I went back home and after breaking the news to my long-suffering wife, two days – and a multitude of jabs – later I was on my way to Zambia. The original plan was for us to go for two weeks, but after racing in Zambia we were then asked to go on to Rhodesia (now Zimbabwe), and finally we were invited to South Africa; five weeks, and a great time later I arrived back home in England."

Following the great welcome he and Malcolm received in southern Africa, Ken would be tempted out of retirement for five more trips up until the mid-1970s, when the curtain finally fell on his long and highly successful trials and scrambles career. He might have hung up his racing leathers, but it's probably fair to say that, to this day, Ken Sedgley has never fully retired from motorcycle sport. He is still actively involved with both motocross and trials through his work with Silkolene, and has just finished restoring a couple of bikes: aptly, a TFS Greeves and a BSA Bantam, which, by the time you read this, he might have ridden in his local club trial.

Big thanks to Ken for all of his help in compiling this profile, and for many happy memories of a golden era in motorcycle sport.

Poise and style on the works Matchless in July 1964. (Courtesy Morton archive)

Whether it was a two- or four-stroke, for over 20 years Vic Eastwood pushed them all to their limits.

CHAPTER 16

VIC EASTWOOD - MULTITASKER

With his distinctive and determined riding style, Vic Eastwood was for over 20 years one of the country's leading scramblers, and a man I first saw racing on a chilly October day at Beenham Park in 1962. It was my first trip to the spectacular Berkshire circuit, but the works AMC man from Kent was by then a regular visitor, and after winning the hard-fought 500cc solo crown two years earlier he came to the start line that day as one of the pre-race favourites. Thousands of fans lined the parkland circuit, and they were in for a treat – not only was Eastwood racing his trusty Matchless, he was also making his debut on the works 250cc two-stroke James.

Scrambles aficionados naturally associated the name of Vic Eastwood with big booming four-strokes, but when the first leg of the 250cc Star got under way he was soon showing his mettle on the lightweight machine. By the end of the first lap he was up with the leading pack, and for eight exciting laps Vic and the little James exchanged places with the two Greeves, ridden by Badger Goss and Roger Snoad. Joe Johnson eventually took the chequered flag, but Eastwood acquitted himself well, and eventually brought the little Villiers-powered two-stroke home in a creditable sixth place.

Later in the day he won the 500c Experts race on his Matchless, but machine troubles saw his retirement from the afternoon's second lightweight race. However, his natural ability to jump from heavyweight four-strokes to lightweight two-strokes was there for all to see, and it marked the prelude to the rest of his highly successful career – 15 glorious years in which his never-say-die riding style made him a firm favourite with both Saturday afternoon TV viewers and a legion of trackside fans the length and breadth of Europe.

During those years – in which he raced factory Matchless, BSAs, Husqvarnas, AJSs, CCM and Maico's – he travelled thousands of miles in pursuit of his championship aspirations, but although there were plenty of memorable victories, he was perhaps one of the best riders of his generation never to wear the British or world crown.

To find out more about his early days, factory bikes, unusual happenings behind the Iron Curtain, and two international six day trials, I spoke to Vic at his home in Kent: a beautiful house that he built in the 1960s, during his days on the works BSA.

That he became a professional scrambler was perhaps not too surprising, as his father was a decent rider himself, and had owned and raced one of the first BSA Gold Stars. It was this bike that whetted his son's appetite for competition.

"Dad had bought and raced the Goldie in Lancashire before he moved south when I was aged about three or four. My first recollections of him racing are when he rode at a Pirbright meeting, and also in the support races of the Motocross Des Nations at Brands Hatch There was a terrific atmosphere at Brands, and it was then I decided that when I was old enough I wanted to race a motorbike. Some time later dad bought me an old three-speed, hand change, girder-forked Francis Barnett which I rode around the car park of his café, but after a while this got rather boring, so feeling adventurous I ventured off-road across the fields and up through the nearby woods.

"This was a lot of fun, but I was keen to race, and in 1956 entered my first scramble. This was on a Greeves which dad had bought me, but unfortunately during practice we were plagued with problems, so the Greeves was sidelined and I ended up racing his 500cc Gold Star. I can't recall the venue, but I remember it was raining hard and the track quickly turned into a quagmire. There was one particularly steep muddy hill which stopped virtually the entire field, but I was fit and strong from playing rugby at school, and thanks to all the practice I'd put in slithering about on my old Franny Barnett in the woods I managed to keep the BSA going and won the race. I still wasn't 16 but I'd managed to get a licence, and this win meant that I was immediately upgraded to Expert status. I figured that racing bikes was much easier than playing rugby, so I decided to finish with the oval ball, dumped the temperamental Greeves, and bought my own 500cc Gold Star."

On leaving school Vic had enrolled at his local polytechnic, and this proved to be a useful environment for turning new bushes for engine rebuilds. By now he was a regular winner on the Kent scrambles scene, and earning some useful money from racing his BSA. Influential people were starting to take notice of the young Eastwood, and a stunning performance at a British Championship race at Hawkstone Park caught the eye of AMC comp shop manager Hugh Viney. Very soon the teenager found himself on a factory Matchless, and any previous thoughts of an engineering degree took a back seat. From then on he spent more time at Woolwich than he did at college, and it was the start of a way of life that would continue for the next 20 years. He told me how it all began.

"I was starting to spread my wings outside the Kent area and managed to get a ride in the British Championship race at Hawkstone Park on my Gold Star. In fact, I surprised myself by finishing fourth behind Johnny Giles, and afterwards I was approached by AMC competition chief Hugh Viney. Viney asked me if I would like to race one of their works Matchless scramblers; better still, he would pay me a retainer, plus I was free to keep any prize money I won, so as you can imagine I didn't take too long to make up my mind."

It was the beginning of a long and successful association with AMC, and Vic was soon notching up some useful wins on the big Matchless. He was also nurturing a good working relationship with the long established members of the comp shop – a team of skilled men who, away from the prying eyes of upper management, carried out a lot of improvements and modifications to the works scramblers.

"Although Hugh Viney was the competition chief, the day to day running of the comp shop was down to Wally Wyatt, Fred Billot, and John McClaren, who between them could get almost anything made or modified, and they were a great bunch to work with.

"When I first joined AMC I was given pretty much a free reign as to what I did, and most of my time at Woolwich was spent working on my own bikes. The 500cc Matchless was a fast machine but it didn't handle too well, so later I went about designing a new Duplex frame. This was drawn out on the floor in chalk, and then I transferred this into metal on a jig. I was particularly pleased with the finished result, as it both went and handled particularly well, and I think I won first time out on it. We soon made another for my team-mate Dave Nicoll, and it was the forerunner of the new generation of very competitive AMC scramblers.

"Spurred on by my wins at home, my dad persuaded me to try to get some rides in the World Championship rounds, and I approached Harold Taylor at the ACU. Harold agreed, and got me an entry in the Italian GP, but as I was an unknown I had to prove myself in qualifying. It was a long drive there in our pick-up truck, but in the pre-race timed practice I did well and finished fourth. As a result of this I came to the start line confident I could mix it with the world's best, but although I managed to get away to a good start I had to pull out at half distance when my chain snapped."

Although Vic was quickly becoming one of the UK's leading scramblers, he readily admits he was no great trials rider and recalls that in his occasional winter time 'wobble' – like a very wet Colmore – he spent more time pushing his C15T up muddy gullies than he did actually riding it.

He did, however, have two rides in the international six days. When I saw him on the James at Beenham in October '62 he'd just returned from Garmisch Partenkirchen in Germany with a prized gold medal. On a works-prepared 497cc AJS – virtually a scrambler with lights - he was selected alongside seasoned six day stars and fellow scramblers Arthur Lampkin and Triss and Bryan Sharp to make up the British Vase B team.

Vic's ISDT debut was a particularly memorable one, as at the end of a muddy week the British team finished runners up to host West Germany in the Silver Vase competition. All four of the team won gold, and after six days and 1200 gruelling miles the Bexley AMC man eventually finished a close second behind experienced Triumph rider Johnny Giles in the individual points tally.

In his eight-page report in the following week's *Motor Cycle*, Harry Louis reported that the Garmisch event was "ideally suited to scramblers," and there was no doubt if they could curb their natural desire to ride flat out, top class riders like Eastwood, Lampkin, and the Sharp brothers were ideally suited to the rigours of the ISDT. The following year Vic was again a member of the Vase B team in Czechoslovakia, but after starting well he crashed and the works AJS was left looking very secondhand. Help was at hand but as he recalled so was an eagle eyed Russian and at the end of the day he was disqualified.

"I was going along at a fair old lick on the Ajay when I was overtaken by a Russian. I did my best to stay with him, but as we crossed a gravel track my back wheel slammed into a stone water viaduct. I stayed on and managed to limp to the next control, but my rear brake hub was badly damaged, and to make matters worse it was a part of the bike which was sealed and couldn't be changed.

"My support crew told me they would be waiting around the next corner to work on it, but in doing so we were spotted by another Russian who reported me and I was subsequently disqualified."

With his ride over, 1963 would be Vic's second and last international six days, and from then on he concentrated all of his efforts

On the works AJS in the Eschen Lake hill climb during the 1962 ISDT. (Courtesy Morton archive)

On the factory BSA in a TV scramble at Leighton in November 1964. (Courtesy Gordon Francis)

into chasing valuable British and World Championship scrambles points on his works Matchless. Travelling the length and breadth of the UK and thousands of miles across Europe racing a motorbike might sound like a romantic way to earn a living, but the combination of driving, racing, and keeping the bikes running was not an easy one.

"Travelling to British and World Championship meetings meant I put thousands of miles a year on my towing vehicles, and although my Matchless was a works machine I had to do most of own mechanical work on it. Racing week in week out was very tiring and I didn't get much rest during the winter either, as I rode in all of the TV scrambles which were usually bitterly cold and muddy. These races were comparatively short so the secret was to get out of the gate as quickly as possible and just go like merry hell."

There was no doubt the armchair fans witnessed some fantastic Saturday afternoon scrambling, and in most events Eastwood and the big Matchless could be found battling for the lead. Vic laughed as he recalled one meeting at Builth Wells where after winning the first leg he fell in the second, but frustratingly was unable to start the big single; the reason, he later discovered, was an exhaust pipe blocked solid with mud.

With his smooth and effortless riding style, an Eastwood crash was a fairly unusual occurrence, but a nasty spill at Hawkstone Park saw him out of action for the best part of two seasons.

"During my career I broke a couple of collar bones in tumbles, but my worst injury came at Hawkstone in a TV event. I'd managed to get away pretty well, but I was blinded by the dazzling sun and failed to negotiate a corner: I couldn't stop and went straight through the ropes and into a tree, badly breaking my knee. This kept me out of action for the best part of two seasons, and when I started racing again I had to modify the footrest, as I couldn't bend my leg back far enough."

By the mid-'60s AMC was in serious financial trouble, and Vic went looking for another works ride. He had the choice of two, and over 40 years later he still reflects as to whether he chose the correct one.

"As I'd witnessed in the World Championship rounds, the works CZ's were both blindingly fast and extremely reliable, so I was left with the decision whether to go with them or a 500cc BSA. This was a similar bike to the one that Smithy had won the world title on, but on reflection I probably made the wrong choice. There was no doubt the Beezer was very fast, but it always felt a bit fragile, and in the heat of racing I had quite a lot of gearbox and clutch problems with it. Third gear would pack up for a pastime, and I recall one event at Builth Wells particularly well – not just because I managed to win both legs, but the frustration of having to strip the box between races only to lose the gear again before I'd completed a couple of laps.

"Things improved when we fitted a Quaife box, and the secret to avoid a slipping clutch was to fit steel plates with no cork. This worked OK but it made it extremely heavy, so once I'd dumped it and cleared the start virtually all of the gear changes were clutchless. Although it wasn't perfect BSA really tried hard, and we would take the bikes to Hawkstone to try out their various modifications and improvements.

"Undoubtedly the best bike I had was a full 500, which featured a longer swinging arm and a special set of 'offset' forks. Made from magnesium, these had a simple hollow tube with a 2.5in slot which allowed the oil to flow through, but even after landing from big jumps they wouldn't bottom out. The only problems we encountered were that the magnesium wore out fairly quickly, but overall it was a superb machine and it was so stable you could ride it with your hands off the bars."

It was a superb machine, and this combined with his undoubted riding skills meant that Eastwood and the BSA briefly led the World Championship standings that year. That was until a simple breakage many miles from home scuppered his title hopes.

"I was having some good rides, and after the fifth round race – in which I finished third – I was actually leading the championships. Unfortunately, at the next round my chain adjuster broke, and the chain jumped the sprockets. I was hundreds of miles from home which meant I couldn't get back to England to get the new parts I needed. I managed to bodge it up, but the uncertainty of whether the chain was going to stay on or not knocked my confidence and I struggled in the next couple of rounds."

Chasing World Championship points took Vic and his family to some fairly inhospitable places, and a trip through the Eastern Bloc in the late '60s was a particularly memorable one.

"It was the height of the Cold War and we set off with the two works BSAs – plus our son Scott in his carrycot – jammed inside my Ford escort estate car. On arrival at the East German border it took ages while they checked our passports and we were given strict instructions as to what roads we were allowed to travel on and where we were permitted to stay overnight. We were very much aware that we were being closely watched wherever we went, but on arrival at the Russian border we were in for a real surprise. We were approached by three men in white suits and one of them – who spoke quite good English – said 'Stop, we must spray you'. Apparently there had been an outbreak of foot and mouth disease in Latvia, and to stop it spreading they were spraying all and sundry with disinfectant. They even wanted us to open our suitcases to spray the contents, but fortunately we managed to discourage them from that. The Russian roads were diabolical and compared to what we were used to at home it was like driving on a dusty and very pot-holed track.

"We'd been joined by a couple travelling in an old Ford Popular, and it was just as well because on one particularly bad stretch of road the Ford got stuck in a huge hole and we had to join forces to lever it clear. Our hotel for the night was certainly very basic, but thankfully the car was locked in the compound overnight and after hours of travelling we eventually arrived at the circuit. The race attracted a huge crowd of around 70,000 people, but it was the middle of summer and the track was incredibly dusty. With temperatures up in the nineties the riding conditions were horrendous, and by the end of the race I was so dehydrated my head was spinning. I don't think I've ever been so hot in all my life. The organising club had thoughtfully erected a massive tent filled with showers, which cooled us down, but basic commodities like drinking water and milk for Scott were difficult to find. Fortunately on our way home we came across a stone trough on the side of the road, so we stopped and filled our water canisters from that."

During the next two seasons there would be numerous victories and other podium finishes for Vic and his BSA, but after a series of breakdowns he became disillusioned with the works 500s, and when his contract ran out he left Small Heath and was signed by Husqvarna importer Brian Leask. It was a shrewd move, and after some initial teething troubles at Matchems that saw him struggling with the floating rear brake on the 250, he quickly adapted to the power delivery of the

Forcing hard on the works Matchless at a Winchester TV scramble. (Courtesy Gordon Francis)

"AFTER WINNING THE FIRST LEG HE FELL IN THE SECOND, BUT FRUSTRATINGLY WAS UNABLE TO START THE BIG SINGLE; THE REASON, HE LATER DISCOVERED, WAS AN EXHAUST PIPE BLOCKED SOLID WITH MUD"

At a very muddy *Grandstand* trophy scramble at Yeo Vale in January 1965. Vic, on the BSA, leads from eventual winner Chris Horsfield.

Swedish two-strokes. He was soon mixing it with the world's best in the 500cc Grands Prix.

"One of my early outings on the Husky was at Namur in Belgium and although I did OK I wasn't totally happy with the handling, so after the meeting Brian Leask went to the factory in Sweden and got me a modified frame. It had a slightly different steering head angle which pushed the forks out slightly but it made the world of difference to the way it handled and steered. In fact, it was so easy you could ride with your hands off the bars. When Brian was at the factory they also gave us a special 440cc barrel and piston, and this transformed a very good bike into a brilliant one. It was extremely fast, and later that season I managed to win both the British and Luxembourg Grands Prix on it."

After two or three highly successful seasons on the Husqvarna, Vic returned to British bikes – firstly a pair of works AJS, and then two years later one of Alan Clews CCMs. I saw him in action on an experimental 500cc AJS at Leighton in April 1972, where he finished third behind Bryan Wade and John Banks. He told me a little about this machine and his subsequent move to CCM.

"The standard 410 AJS was a pretty good bike, but in an effort to keep up with the opposition Peter Inchley and Fluff Brown stretched the engine out to a full 500cc. In ready to race form it had a huge expansion box and a silencer, which not only made it extremely quiet, but also very tractable and easy to ride. I rode it in quite a few British and World Championship rounds, but before it could be developed NVT pulled the plug and I was then signed by Alan Clews to race his BSA-based CCM. With its improved gearbox, stronger clutch and uprated suspension it was everything the works BSA should have been, and I immediately felt at home on it. Vic Allen was the other team rider, and twice a week we would test the bikes in an old sandpit near to my home in Kent. We would keep going for an hour at a time, which gave both us and the bikes excellent preparation for the 45 minutes of a GP, which by comparison were a doddle."

Aviating the 500cc BSA at a TV scramble at Naish Hill, February 1967. (Courtesy Morton archive)

Trackside fans loved the booming four-stroke CCMs, but despite the riders' skills they were hard pushed to keep pace with the lighter, faster two-strokes, and after two or three seasons Vic decided it was a case of 'if you can't beat them, join them,' and signed for Badger Goss' Maico team.

"From my experience of racing against them in the world rounds I knew the Maicos were extremely fast, although I didn't fully appreciate how well they braked and handled until I went with Badger to the factory in Germany. At a casual look they appeared rather crude, but they were extremely rugged, and it only took a quick ride on the factory's test track to realise how good they were."

Vic continued to campaign the German two-strokes in both the British and World Championship rounds for a couple of seasons, but by then he was running a busy motorcycle shop, and he finally retired from racing in the mid-'70s. In addition to the shop – selling mostly Husqvarna and Maico motocrossers – he also found time to develop a power enhancing and quieter exhaust system with DEP, and for many years was a regular sight on his local motocross track, giving the unit a thorough testing.

His retirement brought the curtain down on 20 glorious years of racing. For those of us who were lucky enough to witness him in action, the memories will live forever.

Big thanks to Vic for reliving some of those halcyon days of scrambling.

Vic on the 400cc Husky in the BBC *Grandstand* scramble at Lyng, November 1968. (Courtesy Morton archive)

Blindmoor, 1958. Alan Bell (27), and Paul (1), with Neil holding the Edwards trophy.

Neil Jarman and his brother, Paul, were two of the leading lights in south west centre scrambling in the 1950s, with one of the brothers usually first past the flag.

CHAPTER 17

NEIL & PAUL JARMAN

The Somerton club's event at Steart Hill in February 1961 was described by Ralph Venables as "the muddiest scramble ever held in Somerset." Such were the conditions, few of the 76 entries managed to get further than the end of the start/finish straight before spinning to a halt. However in the glutinous, strength-sapping mud, one young man on a booming BSA Gold Star reigned supreme. His name was Neil Jarman.

Neil won all of the races he'd entered that day, including the second unlimited in which he was the only one of the 32 starters to finish. Unsurprisingly, the following week's *MCN* headlines read "A walkover for Jarman." By then the 26-year-old from Taunton had been racing for ten years and along with his older brother, Paul, he'd become one of the most successful West Country scramblers of his generation. Throughout the 1950s there was barely a south western centre scramble where a Jarman brother wasn't first past the flag, and just for good measure they also became pretty good trials riders, too. Neil was still at his peak when he retired from racing at the end of the 1961 season – Paul had finished 12 months earlier – but nearly half a century on the brothers are still remembered fondly by a legion of West Country fans. When I met up with Neil at his home in the beautiful New Forest in Hampshire, it brought back many happy memories of their all-action style on the big four-strokes.

As I soon discovered, it was hardly surprising that the brothers became top class off-road stars. Before the war their father Frank had competed in many racing disciplines, and when his sons started competing in trials and scrambles it was very much a case of 'a chip off the old block.'

"My dad was a great motorcycle enthusiast, and from an early age he competed in trials, scrambles, hill climbs. He also raced on the road at the old street circuit at Falmouth, and in between times he rode for the Exeter speedway team on a dirt Douglas. Later on he became an ACU steward, and for several years was also president of the south western centre. In 1929 he'd taken over W. P. Edwards Motors in Taunton, so from our earliest days motorcycles were an everyday part of our life.

"Paul was born in August 1932, and I followed in the October two years later. The first bike I can recall riding was dads 350cc BSA when I was aged about 11. I rode it around the field for the whole day without getting out of first gear. There was no schoolboy sport in those days, but as soon as Paul was old enough dad encouraged him to have a go, and in 1948 he started riding in both trials and scrambles on a

Neil at the top of Hawkstone's notorious hill on the 350cc BSA.

350cc BSA. In fact he was still only 17 when dad got him an entry on a 197cc two-stroke factory James in the 1950 international six days trial in Wales."

The records show that Paul survived until day four when he was forced to retire, but in scrambles he had progressed to an Ariel – a bike that featured a McCandless swinging arm frame, and one on which little brother Neil got his first taste of riding on a proper track.

"In the immediate postwar years petrol was rationed, so we ran the Ariel on dope, which made it go really well. At that time I still wasn't old enough to compete myself, so after the day's racing was over I was allowed to tear around the course for a few laps getting a feel of what it was like to ride a bike at speed over rough ground. I had to wait until Boxing Day 1949 to make my race debut at the very muddy Blindmoor circuit – between Chard and Taunton – on a 350cc Triumph: a bike which had previously been burnt out and rebuilt with scrambles knobblies in our workshop. At that time I was still only 15 and a half, but I guess the organisers must have turned a blind eye to that. I can't remember much about the race itself, but I managed to finish and didn't fall off too many times."

It was a one-off ride on the Triumph, as Neil would have to wait until the following March before he raced again, also at Blindmoor, on a 350cc trials Matchless. However, by then he had progressed to riding a BSA on the road.

"I was still at school until June 1951, and I didn't ride in scrambles regularly until the following year, although I did travel to school on a 650cc BSA Gold Flash! Wasn't I lucky?"

During the winter of 1951 he started to ride in trials on the 350 Matchless, but by then big brother Paul was starting to beat some of the West Country's leading scramblers. These included Triumph factory star Jim Alves, who was often left trailing in the wake of the flying Jarman on his McCandless framed Ariel.

"Jim's Triumph had the sprung hub which he described as 'useless' – so useless, in fact, he bolted it up and rode it with a rigid rear end. It might have been an improvement, but he couldn't keep up with Paul, and it came as no surprise when he turned up at the next scramble with the rear of the Triumph covered in a black rubber shroud – this shroud neatly hiding a newly fitted McCandless swinging arm and suspension units on his works Triumph."

On leaving school, Neil joined his big brother in the family motorcycle business. The austere days of the early '50s were some extremely busy ones in the big Taunton shop.

"The business was up and running when dad took it over in 1929 so he never bothered to change its name, but everyone knew it as Jarman's, and we were agents for all of the main British manufacturers of the time. Being the only big town in a largely rural community, many of our customers were farmers who used to turn up on a Saturday afternoon for a look around the showroom. After the tough days of the war it seemed that everyone wanted a motorbike, and typically we would sell a dozen or 15 bikes every Saturday. Nearly everyone wore a tie, and I remember one chap particularly well. He used to come in virtually every week, and irrespective of the weather he always wore a three piece suit and wouldn't dream of donning goggles or gloves."

Many of the customers quickly became trackside fans, but during '52 and '53 there was only one Jarman on the race tracks, as Paul was away in Egypt serving his two years national service. In Neil's words, two 'wasted ones,' serving as a despatch rider dodging lengths of wire which the locals stretched across the sandy roads. While Paul was away, Neil took over his brother's favourite riding number (1) and also the McCandless Ariel, but by now the old 500 single was past its best and it was time to consider a change of machine.

This came about the following season when the Taunton lads wheeled out a pair of brand new 350 and 500cc BSA Gold Stars, and there was soon plenty for their fans to cheer about. Against some top class opposition – including the Sharp and Rickman brothers – the Goldies took the Jarmans to numerous wins on the West Country circuits, although there was plenty of incident and humour along the way.

"Much of our racing was restricted to the south western centre, and the courses at Chard, Blindmoor, and Bridgwater were three of our favourites. Occasionally we would venture farther afield, and one meeting at Walford Cross is particularly memorable. The course itself was very flat – very much like a mountain grass-track – but it had a huge bomb hole in the middle of it. This is where most of the crashes occurred, and I remember one very amusing incident when after a nasty spill the commentator solemnly announced that 'a competitor had broken his arm and racing would be held up while he mended it.' In fact he'd lost his arm in the war, and against all the odds still managed to race with a false one, and it was this which had broken in the fall; 20 minutes later he was repaired and up and racing again."

In January 1953 Neil was called up for his national service, but luckily for him this was as a driver at Thorney Island near Portsmouth. It meant that motorcycling continued unhindered, although it was not without it problems.

"Dad used to transport the bikes on his homemade trailer, which he towed behind a 2.5-litre Riley. Although much of our racing was in the south western centre, we'd entered the Gloucester Grand National and were travelling through Bristol, when suddenly we were overtaken by two scrambles bikes on a trailer. Just to make matters worse, it was our bikes and the trailer tow bar had snapped in half! Fortunately it was a Saturday, so we managed to get to the workshop of our old rival Len Sanders who came out and welded it all back together. Job done, we continued on our way to Gloucester."

Along with Roy Bradley and Doug Dyson, Sanders was one of Bristol's leading scramblers and a tough competitor on the track – but one quick to celebrate when the racing was over for the day.

"It was an era when virtually everyone was racing for the pure fun and enjoyment of it, and if you won it was a bonus. The racing was great and I would often get 'leaned on' by Len or Roy Bradley but at the end of the race we could all sit down and have a good laugh and relive the race in the pub afterwards. There was a great atmosphere to the south western centre events, and some riders like Norman Allen used to travel a long way for their Sunday sport. Norman lived in London, but used to drive over 100 miles to ride. When I asked him why he said it was because he just loved all of the 'nattering' and laughter he found down in the West Country."

That same love of the sport was also carried over into wintertime trials, in which the Jarman brothers often figured in the results. Although by Neil's own admission, Paul was the more talented of the two.

"I think Paul was the better trials rider simply because he had more patience than me, and while I was OK at fast, full bore type sections, he was much better at the nadgery stuff. Time trials were very popular at that time, and I managed to achieve standard [fastest] time in a couple

Neil, feet-up on the trials at Enfield, circa 1959.

"THE COURSE ITSELF WAS VERY FLAT – VERY MUCH LIKE A MOUNTAIN GRASS-TRACK – BUT IT HAD A HUGE BOMB HOLE IN THE MIDDLE OF IT"

Neil leads Roy Bradley (32), brother Paul (1), and Len Sanders (9).

of them, but lost too many marks on observation to win. Of course, it was an era when virtually all trials bikes were big four-strokes, and after riding the 350cc Matchless a couple of times I soon progressed to a 500T Norton. This was followed by a swinging arm 500cc BSA – a lovely machine – and then by a 350cc royal Enfield, which I rode right up to when I retired from trials in 1963. Paul rode in the Scottish six days a couple of times with Jim Alves, but it was impossible for both of us to be away from the shop at the same time, so as he was the better rider he got to go to the Highlands and I stayed at home. He also did a few of the trade-supported nationals, but the trouble was they were always on Saturday, which was our busiest day, so most of our trials action was limited to open-to-centre events on Sundays."

Difficulty getting away from the shop on Saturdays also restricted their appearances in the British Championship scrambles rounds, but the skills they'd achieved sliding around the big four-strokes came in very useful when they rode in the 1956 Welsh three-day trial.

"Paul had already ridden in Wales in the 1950 ISDT, and we'd also driven to Varese in Italy in dad's Riley to spectate at the following year's international, so in 1956 we decided to do the Welsh.

"The ideal bike for the Welsh three days was a scrambler with trials tyres, but I entered on a 350cc trials BSA, which was still on its original low trials gearing. The event gave both me and the bike one hell of a bashing, and at the end of the three days I'd worn out both front and rear tyres, the brake linings, and the drive chain. I had to ride the bike virtually flat out for the whole time, and after jumping over a bridge I was stopped by a policeman who asked me if I was in a 'race.' All I could say was yes. He raised his eyebrows and sent me on my way. I've got a feeling that Bob Manns was overall victor that year, but Paul won the 250cc Cup and I managed a first-class award."

Many of the Jarmans' scrambles successes were achieved on the big bangers, but they also had some memorable rides in 1957 on a brace of lightweight Greeves two-strokes, which Neil recalled were like toys compared to the huge 500cc Gold Stars. Although Saturday work commitments at the Taunton shop prevented them from riding in the British Championship rounds, the brothers were selected to ride for the south west in the inter-centre team event, and soon proved they were more than capable of mixing it with the best.

"We rode at Matchem's Park – too sandy and stony – and also at Hawkstone, but undoubtedly one of my best rides was in the 1959 inter-centre team scramble at Shrublands Park, where I managed to finish sixth. I was riding number ten, which was very apt because it was ten days after Ann and I had got married, and I had to interrupt our honeymoon to go scrambling."

The late '50s saw the Jarman brothers at their best, with Paul winning the prestigious Patchquick trophy in Devon, and Neil finishing third behind Don and Derek Rickman at George Pickett's farm at Exmouth. They also figured in the results in the 350cc class at the annual Sunbeam club's point to point, against a field of established star riders.

"We weren't particularly well established nationally, so many of the crowd and fellow competitors were surprised to see a couple of 'unknowns' dicing with the works-supported riders. At the end of the race in which Paul was third and I was fifth, I heard Terry Cheshire asking someone 'Who was that bloke who kept getting in my way? I couldn't get past him.' The reply was simply 'That was Paul Jarman.'"

In addition to the old faithful Goldies, Neil also raced a 500cc TriBSA for a while, the handling of which was a revelation after the rather ponderous BSA.

"The Gold Star – which was available as trials, scrambler and clubman's racer – was a fantastic machine, but it was a lump, and after heavy landings in scrambles the fork tubes had a tendency to bend. After every third or fourth meeting we used to turn them in the yolks, but they soon bent again, which meant throwing them away. The TriBSA was a 500cc Triumph engine housed in a BSA frame with Norton forks and front brake, so not only did it go well it also stopped and handled with equal aplomb."

The following season saw the brothers revert to a pair of works-supported Goldies, and in September 1960 Neil made his long-awaited debut ride in France.

"Bryan Sharp had entered a couple of events in France, but as he was unable to go I took over his ride. At that time Ann was seven-and-a-half months pregnant, and we travelled to the two meetings along with the two partially dissembled bikes inside Arthur Harris' Peugeot estate car. We raced at Argentan and also at the famous old chalk pit circuit at Montreuil in the suburbs of Paris. Before the racing started we were encouraged to ride through the streets in convoy making as much noise as we liked to draw the crowds, who arrived in their thousands. The tracks were very different to those at home, but I had a couple of good rides, finishing third in race one and fourth in the second leg. The races were just a week apart, so in between times we had a week's holiday in Paris – six weeks later our son, Ian, was born."

In October of 1960, Neil once again lined up with Terry Cox, Brian Slee, and John Tribble for the south western in the team event at Wick Farm, Glastonbury. However, in the same month Paul decided to call it a day. There would be plenty more wins for Neil during the 1961 season, but with a young family and pressure of work, he too hung up his leathers 12 months later. The brothers' retirement brought the curtain down on a memorable decade, but for those who were lucky enough to witness them in action, the memories of the Jarman brothers and their booming BSAs will live forever.

Paul passed away in 2001, but I'm indebted to Neil for all of his time and hospitality in reliving some of the halcyon days of motorcycle sport.

Neil on the TriBSA at an Exmoor scramble at Lynton, 1959

Neil aviates the TriBSA at Glastonbury Tor, circa 1960

Plenty of body lean from Pat on the 197cc James in the Oxford Cup trial.

One of the stars of the '60s off-road scene, Pat Lamper's name was often near the top of the race result sheets – particularly if the rain arrived and the ground became swamp-like.

CHAPTER 18

PAT LAMPER – MASTER OF THE MUD

The 13th annual Sunbeam point-to-point in April 1959 was regarded as the wettest on record, and when racing started, the circuit – which had previously been described as 'smooth and fast' – quickly developed into a muddy morass. With the rain pouring down, the steep slopes at the top of the course brought many riders slithering to a halt, but one who revelled in the grim conditions was a young man on a works Dot. His name was Pat Lamper.

8000 rain-soaked fans witnessed the racing that day, and at the end of 16 slippery laps Pat took the winner's flag ahead of Mike Jackson and Brian Stonebridge on their factory Greeves. With skills he'd developed from riding in trials, Lamper was by then regarded as a 'master of the mud,' and in a career that lasted over 20 years he became one of the best 250cc riders of his generation. I first saw him and the screaming Dot in action at a windy Beenham Park in October 1962 where, after some memorable dices with Joe Johnson, Badger Goss, and Don Rickman, he ran out overall winner of the British 250cc Championship races. With a thrilling day's racing at an end, I made the long journey back to Somerset in the back of my big brother's A40 van. Little then could I have imagined that 46 years later I would be interviewing the same man, and sharing memories from those great days of scrambling.

Born in Horsham Sussex in 1936, Pat was in his early teens when he saw his first scramble, and it wasn't long before he entered his first event.

"My dad had no interest in motorcycles, but I became hooked after my friend's father – who was a great enthusiast – took us in his sidecar to nearby Oxford to watch a scramble. For me it started my passion for bikes, and on leaving school I was keen to become a motorcycle mechanic, but my father poured cold water on the idea and persuaded me to become an agricultural engineer. I soon discovered it to be very boring and stuck at it for about six months, until I saw John Avery was looking for an apprentice in his bike shop in Oxford. I applied and was lucky enough to be taken on.

"It was 1951, and I'd already ridden in my first trial on a BSA Bantam, and in the same year I also got a surprise outing on my boss's works scrambler. John was riding in the British GP at Hawkstone, and after the racing was over he asked me if I'd like to ride his Gold Star around the circuit. The descent from the big hill was a bit hairy, but I guess I must have done OK, because on our return he sorted me out with a rigid 350cc BSA and I entered my first scramble. This was at Midgham near Newbury, and dad took the bike on a trailer behind his

1958 inter-centre team scramble at Brill. Pat on the 500cc BSA.

On a 500cc BSA Gold Star at Beenham Park in 1958.

Hillman Minx car. I remember it was pouring down with rain, which made the going extremely muddy, but I stayed on and managed to finish first in the novices' race. It was great to start with a win, so I began racing regularly on the BSA, and around that time I also had a go at sidecar scrambles – not riding but acting as passenger to the American George White, and also a few times to Pip Barrett on his BSA twin."

Pat's career as sidecar ballast was short-lived. In both trials and scrambles, a change of machine had seen him upgraded to Expert status.

"I pensioned off the Bantam and changed it for a 197cc James, which I rode to events all across the South Midlands centre. It was a good little bike and I started to pick up a few awards in open-to-centre trials. In 1954 my dad also bought me a new 500cc Gold Star scrambler – this was a fantastic machine compared to the rigid 350, and within six months I was upgraded to Expert."

At that time the South Midlands centre was a hotbed of trials and scrambles talent, and every weekend during the summer Pat was racing against the likes of Andy Lee, Dave Curtis, Joe Johnson and Frank Underwood – riders who, along with Lamper, would later represent their centre in the inter-centre team races.

During 1955 and '56 Pat rode the 500cc Gold Star to numerous scrambles wins, but his wintertime trials skills had also become noticed. Following a recommendation to Small Heath, 1957 saw him mounted on an ex-John Draper works BSA.

"Ralph Venables had a lot of influence within the factory competition circles, and it was thanks to him I got the ex-Draper BSA. The same year I also got called up for my two year's national service, but as I soon discovered Ralph was very good at pulling a few strings in military circles too, so I knew exactly where I was going. I did a few weeks at Blandford Forum, and then moved on to Norton Fitzwarren near Taunton for my trade training. It meant that I could still ride in scrambles, and every weekend my dad used to bring the bike down for me to race against some of the south western stars, including the Jarman brothers and Terry Cox. Later I was transferred to Boredon in Hampshire, where I was posted to the sixth training battalion, and then into the motorcycle section with Pat Brittain. Most of our time there was spent teaching second lieutenants from Sandhurst to ride their bikes, two weeks training them on- and off-road, which was a huge amount of fun.

"Most Wednesday's we also competed in group trials riding against the navy, RAF, army and police, and thanks to our commanding officer – Captain Davey – we even had our own Nissan hut to prepare our civvy bikes in. We were given loads of time off, and were told we could go and ride wherever we liked as long as it wasn't in a communist country."

Thanks to Venables' influence, Pat was able to return home every weekend, so there was no interruption to his motorcycling career. As he told me, '57 was proving to be a good year.

"With Brian Stonebridge in their ranks, Greeves were starting to challenge Dot as the leading two-strokes and I signed up to ride for them – incidentally, on the same day as a young lad from East Anglia: Dave Bickers. Two-stroke tuning was still a bit of a 'black art,' but during his time at BSA 'Strawberry' had done a lot of work with Herman Meier, and his Greeves was starting to go really well. In addition to the Greeves I still had my Gold Star, and was also riding an Army issue 350cc Matchless in their trials."

Pat became very adept at riding the heavyweight Matchless – a bike formerly ridden by Johnny Giles – and in October 1959 he won the tough championship trial at Catterick, where he was not only best national serviceman, but also best overall.

After 12 months with Greeves, Pat signed for its northern rival, Dot. His race debut came in the Experts Grand National in July 1958. In the 250cc race he was soon dicing for the lead with his ex-Thundersley team-mate Brian Stonebridge, but in a spirited attempt to overtake, his front wheel touched Stonebridge's rear tyre, and Lamper stepped off, leaving the Greeves man to take the chequered flag ahead of Triss Sharp on a Francis Barnett, and John Harris on another Greeves.

It was the start of a long association between Lamper and the Manchester made two-strokes, and that famous win in the Sunbeam point-to-point would be the first of many. For the 1960 season Pat lined up alongside Alan Clough and Ken Messenger as the works scrambles riders, and also as a member of the ten-strong trials team. The same year also saw him move to Ellesmere Street to work. He told me how that came about, and about the set-up at the Hulme factory.

"I came out the army in June 1960 and went back to my old job as a mechanic at John Avery's, but later that year I landed a position with Dot in Manchester. On the bumpy northern circuits the Dots had the handling advantage, but on the smooth southern courses they were struggling to keep up with the faster Greeves, and I was having all sorts of trouble with the gearbox. I was getting really fed up, so my father suggested that I should take some time off from Avery's and 'go up and sort them out.' I was only there about a week when Mr Burnard Wade offered me the job of assistant works manager/comp shop manager: one which I soon found out was a bit of everything.

"The Ellesmere Street works was a three-storey building – quite a small place – which I was told had formerly been a cotton mill, and not the sort of place you would expect to find a motorcycle factory. The total workforce was only about 15 or 16 people, and I looked after all of the works bikes in my 'comp shop' workshop on the ground floor. The ground floor was also home to the frame building and machine shop, while the 'assembly line' was on the third floor, which meant that when they were finished the bikes had to be lowered to the ground by a winch, which was all a bit crude."

Burnard Wade had taken over at the ailing Dot factory in 1932, and was considered a good boss, but as Pat soon discovered, the little Manchester company was a microcosm of the British motorcycle industry as a whole.

"Mr Wade was a nice chap, but he didn't move with the times, and he steadfastly refused to change anything to make the bikes more reliable. The gears in the standard Villiers box had a rough time on a scrambler, and often during racing I would lose third and would have to strip the gearbox between a heat and a final. It was an ongoing problem, but he never did anything about it, and any alterations that were done were usually scribbled on the back of a cigarette packet. At that time Alan Clough, John Griffiths, and myself were the works scrambles team, but our bikes were exactly the same specification as those sold to the public. In fact, Mr Wade insisted on it. I had three works bikes, two of which I kept in the comp shop and the other one – with all of the go faster parts on it – at home, which he didn't get to see. Undoubtedly the best bike I had was one with a Vale Onslow barrel and expansion chamber which ran on methanol. This was really quick, but we weren't allowed to run it on methanol in the nationals, so reverting back to petrol any advantage was lost."

Trials action from the Kickham, 14 March, 1959, on a 350cc BSA.

Dicing with Vic Eastwood on his 250cc Matchless.

Despite the shortcomings of the scrambler, the trials bikes were still extremely competitive, and in January of 1960 Pat notched up first-class awards in the Vic Brittain, Musketeers and St David's, and also achieved best performance in the muddy Hampshire Rose. There were also successful rides in the Scottish six days (first-class award) and the tough Scott time and observation trial, but it was in scrambles that the name of Lamper was spread to a wider audience, in the Saturday afternoon televised events. Burnard Wade might have been slow to introduce changes, but in January 1962 Pat wheeled out the new scrambler and promptly finished second to John Burton's works BSA in the televised 250cc race. With its Marcelle conversion and an all-new welded frame, Pat quoted it as "performing 25 per cent better than the previous model," with "excellent racing characteristics."

With the bike on a trailer made from Dot fork tubes he covered thousands of miles in pursuit of championship points, and also spread his wings to continental meetings – although this was not with his boss' blessing.

"Before I'd joined Dot I'd raced in Switzerland in 1956 – I won the first race but retired in the second with an oiled plug – and I also scooped the international 250cc Irish motocross in Dublin two years on the trot. I recall that my first 'home' GP was at Beenham Park, and it was the first time I'd seen a Jawa/CZ. They looked very much like a glorified road bike, but were blindingly fast and in the races they left us standing."

Later in the '60s Dot's Burnard Wade actually made a few bikes powered by CZ engines, and they were extremely competitive. John Griffith's raced one for a season, and it proved to be a very fast and reliable little machine. On the home front Pat never finished out of the top five in the important trade-supported nationals and British Championship rounds, but his desire to spread his wings to the international stage fell on deaf ears at Ellesmere Street.

"I loved racing in the GPs – perhaps my best ride was when I finished fifth at Midgham – but when I approached Burnard Wade about competing in the series he just wasn't interested. Along with Jack Matthews and Ken Sedgley I later got to ride in Belgium, France, and Ireland, but we had to fund all the entries and travelling ourselves."

With his smooth and controlled riding style, Lamper rarely crashed. However, he recalled an incident at the national Cotswold scramble from which he was lucky to escape without serious injury.

"Although on the fast circuits the Dot was a bit short of performance, it was very robust, and other than an occasional broken spoke a breakage was something very unusual. As had already been proven by Bill Barugh in the '50s, the little two-strokes were more than capable of taking on and beating the bigger four-strokes, so they made me a 350cc to try out. I entered it in the national Cotswold, and I was going pretty well until I jumped through a gateway into a field, when all of a sudden I went sprawling. I staggered to my feet and looked at the bike which was lying on the ground with the forks detached from the frame. On landing, the jolt had snapped the steering head in half and the bottom of the frame had dug into the ground. It was hardly my fault, but for some reason Dot went mad that I'd broken their new bike."

Throughout the '60s Pat continued to notch up numerous wins in both trials and scrambles. He rode regularly for the north in the annual race against the south, and during his career also tried his hand at both grass-tracking and speedway.

"As a lad I did a lot of cycle speedway, which was very popular at the time, and in the late '50s I also raced in a few grass-tracks on my scrambler. In fact, I managed to win a heat at an event near Dorchester in 1957. I tried out a speedway bike at Belle Vue in Manchester and loved it, but as I was riding in either a scramble or trial every weekend I just didn't have the time to pursue it."

After five happy and hugely successful years, Pat left Dot in 1965, and the following season raced a new Greeves Challenger. On the Thundersley two-stroke he quickly proved he was still a force to be reckoned with, and there was rarely a quarter-litre scramble where the names of Lamper and Greeves didn't feature in the results. Success on the Greeves brought him to the attention of the UK's Maico importer, Tom Jones, who signed him to ride the German two-strokes in January 1966. Pat took over the bike previously tried by John 'Burly' Burton, and at the time was Maico's only sponsored rider in the UK. Some of the 'continentals' had already shown that the Maico was a seriously competitive machine, and in March 1966 Pat and Jones took a pair of 250 and 360cc engines to the factory to pick up some tuning tips. This quickly paid dividends, and despite some teething problems 1967 was a successful season – one that culminated in September when, aboard the Maico, Pat captained the north to victory against the 'old enemy' from the south.

It was Pat's last scramble. On 1 October 1967, he and his business partner Joe Douglas took over a garage at Tickenham, buying, selling, and repairing bikes and cars. Not that this was the end of his competition career – he continued to ride in trials on a Greeves, later progressed to a Bultaco, and represented his new Wessex centre in the inter-centre team trial. He also tried his hand at sidecar trials, and with his stepdaughter in the chair – described by Pat as a natural – he mixed it with the West Country's best until at the age of 54, when he eventually called it a day.

Pat is now retired from his garage business, but is still extremely fit and active, and lives in Clevedon, north Somerset with his wife, Valerie. Pat Lamper was undoubtedly one of the best scrambles and trials riders of his generation, and for this ten-year-old from Frome, the sight and sounds of that day at Beenham Park in 1962 will live forever.

Big thanks to Pat for his hospitality and help in compiling this profile.

Twesledown, Hants, 1965. Pat leads Bill Gwyne.

“MY DAD ALSO BOUGHT ME A NEW 500CC GOLD STAR SCRAMBLER – THIS WAS A FANTASTIC MACHINE COMPARED TO THE RIGID 350, AND WITHIN SIX MONTHS I WAS UPGRADED TO EXPERT”

On the 250cc Maico at Nantwich, 1967.

Also from Veloce –

ISBN: 978-1-84584-159-1

Hardback • 20.7x25cm • £29.99* UK/$59.95* USA • 160 pages • 167 colour and b&w pictures

THE definitive book of the BSA Bantam, a simple commuter bike that thousands learnt to ride on. The book includes year-by-year specifications, colour schemes and engine/frame numbers. Also contains a guide to buying a secondhand Bantam and details of Bantam clubs and specialists. The essential Bantam companion!

For more info on Veloce titles, visit our website at www.veloce.co.uk • email: info@veloce.co.uk • Tel: +44(0)1305 260068
* prices subject to change, p&p extra

INDEX

82